Mafia Men

Gene Hatcher

Published by Trellis Publishing, 2021.

MAFIA MEN

First edition. July 1, 2021.

Copyright © 2021 Gene Hatcher.

ISBN: 979-8224886371

Written by Gene Hatcher.

MAFIA MEN

GENE HATCHER

DANNY GREENE

One of the Midwest's most notorious organized crime figures, Danny "The Irishman" Greene started out with various criminal operations – gambling, racketeering, and loan-sharking – and earned himself a coveted spot as a mob strongman. Still, Greene managed to avoid facing real persecution up until his death in 1977, which has triggered speculation that he might have also worked as an FBI informant.

A struggle from day one

First generation Irish-American immigrants John Henry Greene and Irene Cecilia Fallon were only twenty years old when their son was conceived. After a shotgun wedding before a justice of the peace on November 9, 1933, the couple welcomed their son just five days later – November 14, 1933.

Just a few days after the child was born, Irene passed away due to complications resulting from an enlarged heart. The baby wasn't even given a name until after Irene's burial, but John Greene eventually settled on Daniel – after the newborn's paternal grandfather.

John had worked as a traveling salesman for Fuller Brush, but after his wife passed away, he began to drink heavily. When he lost his job, he moved in with his recently widowed father, who was a newspaper printer. John struggled to provide for his infant son and sent him to a Roman Catholic orphanage called Parmadale.

Greene started attending St. Jerome Catholic School, where he was well-liked by the nuns and priests despite his frequent misbehavior in class. Although he didn't earn good grades, he was dedicated student – serving as an altar boy and a key member of the school's basketball team. He was such a valuable player that he was allowed to play sports even with his poor academic performance.

By 1939, Greene's father had gotten himself back on track. He remarried and started a family with his new wife, but Greene didn't care for his new stepmother. After running away from home several times, Greene was eventually taken in by his maternal grandmother and his aunt, who cared for him until his adolescence. In 1959, when John Green died, an obituary in the local newspaper recognized only the children from his second marriage – there was nothing about his first-born son.

Greene continued to struggle through his education at St. Ignatius High School, where he first encountered racism from Italian-American students – racism that would fuel his lifelong hatred of Italians. The students mocked his Irish heritage, and the confrontations would often end infighting. Eventually, Greene was expelled from St. Ignatius and transferred to Collinwood High School.

At Collinwood, Greene's athletic abilities enabled him to excel in extracurriculars, and he also got involved with the Boy Scouts of America. However, he was kicked out of the organization after only a short time, and he was expelled from Collinwood due to his excessive tardiness, primarily a result of the frequent bullying he endured from other students.

The Celtic warrior

Thanks to his love of physical activity, Greene was always very fit – and he was incredibly self-conscious about his appearance. His usual workouts included running and weight lifting, and as he got older, he became even more rigid with his entire lifestyle. He quit smoking, stopped drinking, and began sticking to a diet of vegetables, fish, and vitamin supplements.

In 1951, following his expulsion from Collinwood, Greene enlisted in the United States Marines. Immediately, he was recognized as a capable boxer and an excellent marksman before being sent to Jacksonville, North Carolina, to serve on Marine Corps Base Camp Lejeune after his induction.

He was transferred after only a few weeks, however, and wound up being shipped to a number of camps over the next few years – possibly as a result of his ongoing behavioral issues. Despite this, Greene was well-respected in the Marines. By 1953, he'd earned a promotion to the rank of corporal, and began training new recruits to use artillery. Later that year, Greene was honourably discharged.

Greene found a job working as a longshoreman on the Cleveland docks, before the International Longshoremen's Association began monopolizing the industry. Whenever he had spare time, Greene could be found researching Ireland, his ancestral homeland. The history of the Celts intrigued and impressed him, and Greene would often look for ways to model his behavior after these ancient warriors. Some have speculated that Greene's ongoing obsession with his heritage may have contributed to his later criminal ambitions.

In his continued celebration of his noble Irish heritage, Greene often wore green clothes and painted the walls of his office the same hue. He is also remembered as having driven green cars, wearing a green crucifix around his neck, and even signing his name with green ink.

Greene worked his way up to become a union organizer and, eventually, became a union boss – he ran for office in the longshoremen's union Local 1317 in 1961 and was elected president. He provided a strong voice to the dockworkers, but behind the scenes, he was a bit of a scam artist.

Before they would earn a position working on the docks, Greene would force new longshoremen to work "temporarily," unloading grain from the boats before handing their paychecks over to Greene. While Greene claimed the money was supporting a future union hall facility, the majority wound up in his personal bank account.

"He imagined himself a tough dock boss," claimed one unidentified union member, years later. "But he was thirty years too late. He used workers to beat up union members who did not come in line, but he was never seen fighting himself. He was a spellbinding speaker and a good organizer."

Occasionally, Greene would shut the docks down, sometimes up to twenty-five times a day – just to show company owners the powerful authority he held over the workers. He's even said to have threatened to kill the children of one of these company owners, who had to seek FBI protection for his house and have armed U.S. Marshals escort his son and daughter to and from school.

In 1966, Greene faced his first criminal trial after he was caught embezzling funds from the International Longshoremen's Association. The trial lasted seven weeks, and according to retired assistant U.S. attorney Donald K. Cimino, Greene knew how to charm the jury.

"Mr. Greene was – let me find the appropriate expression – very aware he was in a U.S. District Court," Cimino said. "He was very adroit at adjusting himself to the atmosphere."

Cimino described Greene as "neat, clean, and well-mannered," who rose respectfully each time the jury or court entered and left. Despite Greene's learned politeness, though, Cimino said his eyes gave him away.

"If you looked into his eyes," Cimino said, "you knew you were dealing with a strong-arm man."

Although Greene had been convicted of embezzling more than $11,000 from the association, he managed to have the conviction reversed on appeal – claiming there had been a prejudicial cross-examination on behalf of the government. As a result, Greene pled guilty to the charge of violating union laws and was only required to pay a $10,000 fine – a fine he didn't end up paying.

He had lost his standing with the union, though, and started looking for work that would be more understanding of his criminal tendencies.

Keeping the peace

Soon after he began working with the Cleveland Solid Waste Trade Guild organizing trash haulers, reports began to circulate that Greene was feuding with a hauler named Michael W. Frato, who had left Greene's guild.

The two used to be close partners – so close, in fact, that each had a son named after the other. However, "Big Mike" Frato wanted to start a legitimate trade group, to be called the Cuyahoga County Refuse Haulers Association, and took issue with the mob involvement Greene was bringing to the guild.

Greene had apparently been brought on by Cleveland family boss Frank "Little Frank" Brancato as muscle, to enforce the mafia's influence over garbage hauling contracts. Along with several other Irish gangsters, Greene was supposed to "keep the peace" – but wound up doing very much the opposite. Brancato openly admitted that bringing Greene into the mod was something he deeply regretted, up until his death in 1973.

According to some sources, one of Greene's own associates started leaking information to Frato – and when Greene's man Arthur Sneperger was attempting to plant a bomb on Frato's car, it suddenly went off, killing him in the explosion. Despite Greene's statements expressing grief and surprise, police were convinced Greene had organized the bomb's detonation to eliminate Sneperger, who may have been the source of the leaked information.

"It wasn't an accident," a Celtic Clubber was quoted as saying. "Artie was a snitch. He was talking to everybody, and we did him in. Remote control."

Sneperger was also revealed to be a police informant, who spilled the details of Greene's mob activity to Sgt. Edward Kovacic with the Cleveland Police Intelligence unit – including the fact that Greene was working as an informant for the FBI.

In 1971, Greene was out for a run when Frato pulled up next to him, as a passenger in the car. According to reports from investigators, he pointed his gun in Greene's face and told him, "I've got you now!"

Greene, however, immediately dropped to the ground and drew his own pistol, which he shot in the direction of the vehicle. Frato took the bullet in the head and was dead before his driver reached Mount

Sinai Hospital. Greene was charged with manslaughter as a result but was acquitted on the grounds of self-defense.

Soon after, he landed himself a job as an enforcer for Jewish mobster Alex "Shondor" Birns. According to Cleveland Plain Dealer reporter Terence Sheridan, a former Cleveland private investigator, Birns was known as the "toughest Jew in town." However, he had taken a liking to Greene, and was even overheard telling someone that Greene was "a mick and a little hotheaded, but he's like a son to me."

Still, this wasn't enough for Greene, who began operating other criminal outfits and earning himself the title of "the king of Cleveland racketeering" among Cleveland police. He'd moved to Collinwood shortly after Frato's attempt on his life, leaving his wife and two daughters behind, and was keeping himself busy by ensuring the neighborhood "undesirables" were under control.

He'd also begun developing his own crew – young, Irish-American gangsters who called themselves The Celtic Club. This included Keith Ritson, Kevin McTaggart, Brian O'Donnell, Danny Greene Jr., Billy McDuffy, and James "Icepick" Sterling. He eventually built an alliance with Cleveland racketeer John Nardi, who was seeking to overthrow the current Cleveland family mafia leadership.

According to Lt. Andrew S. Vanyo, head of Cleveland's criminal intelligence unit, Greene was running legitimate businesses, including land speculation, in addition to his criminal pursuits. Many organized crime figures started viewing Greene as competition, especially when he started taking over some of Birns' operations after his boss was incarcerated.

Mounting tension

Birn had loaned Greene $75,000 to set up a "cheat spot" – a speakeasy and gambling house – through his connections with the Gambino crime family. However, the establishment was never developed, as the cash wound up with a numbers operator named Billy Cox, who apparently used the funds to fuel his narcotics habit. His home was raided by Cleveland police, who seized the drugs and the remaining cash after arresting Cox.

When the Gambino family began pressing Birns for a repayment on the loan, Greene refused to give him the money back, claiming that the loss of the $75,000 loan wasn't his fault. But Birns wasn't about to be taken advantage of and had already left $25,000 in the hands of an associate, with instructions to take out a hit on Greene in the event of any harm coming to Birns.

Moving target

Greene's quest for power and his threatening presence in Cleveland's organized crime network led to many attempts on his life – and he chalked up his uncanny ability to evade his assailants by claiming it was simply the "luck of the Irish."

"He was larger than life," said historian Rick Porrello, who wrote a book about Greene's life. "Very charismatic, very bold. The people hired to kill him didn't want to get too close. He had this air of invisibility."

Shots were apparently fired through the windows of Greene's house sometime in 1968, but the matter was never resolved. He also survived a bombing attack on the apartment building where he was living with his girlfriend. He'd been on the second floor of his suite and wound up breaking several ribs when he landed on a pile of debris. Both Greene and his girlfriend, Denise, were alright, but two of Greene's cats were killed in the blast.

"I felt the floor give out," Greene recalled. "The next thing I knew, I was in a heap of rubble. An icebox was over me. I dug myself out. I heard dogs whining and cats crying."

According to reports, a second bomb had been planted in the building but had somehow failed to detonate during the explosion. Had this bomb also gone off, the blast would have certainly killed Greene – and to Greene, this miraculous occurrence was all thanks to St. Jude, whose medal could always be found around Greene's neck.

There was also an explosion in Greene's green Cadillac. The bomb squad's initial determination was that the explosion was an accident, that Greene had carelessly set off a bomb intended for a rival. According to Greene, a car had pulled up next to him and someone had thrown the bomb into his back seat, adding that he couldn't understand why anyone would be picking on him.

However, when the bomb squad tried to validate their suspicions that the bomb had been Greene's, they claimed he refused to answer.

"What's that you say?" Greene supposedly told them. "The bomb hurt my ears and I can't hear you."

According to Vanyo, Greene was thought to have been involved in nearly 80 percent of Cleveland bombings in the ten years leading up to his death. He had also told police that he wasn't afraid of dying. Vanyo described Greene as "formidable and dangerous."

In Porrello's account of Greene's life, he claimed Greene had "personally assassinated" at least eight of the would-be Mafia assassins sent to take his life – primarily through bombs and bullets.

"The luck of the Irish is with me," Greene once said to a reporter during a televised interview, "and I have a message for those yellow maggots (Cleveland mafia). That includes the payers and the doers. The doers are the people who carried out the bombing – they have to be eliminated because the people who paid them can't afford to have them remain alive. And the payers are going to feel great heat from the FBI and the local authorities."

He added that he wanted to "clear up" the misconception that he'd been running away from the explosion – "I walked away," he said.

Greene is also suspected of killing much of his competition – including Birns, who was killed in March of 1975 when he got into his car outside of a Cleveland church and a bomb exploded. Greene was also a primary suspect in the 1976 bombing of Eugene J. Ciasullo, who was in the hospital for three weeks to treat chest injuries resulting from the shrapnel in the bomb.

"He knew the code: those who live by the bomb die by the bomb," said Vanyo. "He had always told me that when he went, it would be by a bomb, not a shooting."

Trojan Horse

Vanyo wasn't wrong. Greene was killed by a car bomb himself, on October 6, 1977.

"There were lots of odors, like burning rubber, material from the car," said Sara Peck, who was working as a teller at the St. Clair Savings Association when she heard the explosion and ran into the street to see what had happened.

"I looked at him. It was like a wax dummy," she said.

According to investigators, a bomb had been planted in a parked car adjacent to the late-model Continental Greene was using, and as he attempted to enter the vehicle after a visit to the dentist, the bomb was detonated by someone watching nearby. The same "Trojan Horse" bombing style had been used earlier that year to kill John Nardi.

"Somebody knew he had a dentist's appointment," Vanyo said. "Somebody knew what kind of car he was driving."

Vanyo said Greene and his associate Keith Ritson both drove Lincoln Continentals, and frequently switched vehicles to confuse their enemies. According to Vanyo, the attack was a "set up" – the possibility of someone following Greene around with a car full of explosives was very unlikely.

Greene's body remained under the red Nova that had contained the bomb for at least an hour as more than twenty investigators combed the scene for every scrap of evidence. His arm, torn from the body and thrown 100 feet away, still had a gold ring on one of the fingers – adorned with five green stones.

The Nova had been registered to a man named Henry Rollin, who was no longer living at the address listed on the registration. Investigators didn't have much to say about the bombing that killed Greene, but one was quoted as saying, "I think we can safely assume

Danny was not hit for spitting on the sidewalk. He was a very neat fellow."

According to Terence Sheridan, a former Cleveland private investigator, the attack was carried out by the Italian mafia – who knew Greene had been working as an FBI informant under the code name Mr. Patrick. Sheridan said Greene had developed a relationship with another Irishman, FBI Special Agent Martin McCann, during his trial for embezzlement.

"He covered his back and snitched on the Italians," Sheridan wrote in a 2011 tribute to Greene which ran in the Cleveland Plain Dealer. "Unfortunately, McCann didn't know that while the FBI was wiretapping the Italians, the Italians were wiretapping the Irishman – and they knew exactly when he would be visiting his dentist in October 1977."

Lasting legacy

Greene's murder led to more than 20 different convictions within the Cleveland mob circuit, with nine men indicted initially thanks to eyewitness accounts. The trial lasted 79 days, from February to May 1978 – the longest running continuous criminal trial Cuyahoga County had ever seen.

The murder, and Greene's life, also provided further inspiration for a number of books. In 1998, historian Rick Porrello penned "To Kill the Irishman: The War That Crippled the Mafia" – a book which was eventually adapted for the big screen. 2011's Kill the Irishman starred Ray Stevenson as Greene, Christopher Walken as Birns, and Vincent D'Onofrio as Nardi.

The film follows Greene's life, beginning with his childhood in Collinwood and leading up to his election as president of the Longshoremen's union in the early 1960s. However, the story provides deeper insight into Greene's confrontations with the Cleveland mafia throughout the 1970s.

"So many times, Hollywood screenwriters are asked to do a real-life story but to inject false elements in order to make the lead character more likable," said Jonathan Hensleigh, who both directed and co-wrote the film. "We didn't have to do that with Danny Greene."

Despite the violence Greene had no doubt inflicted on many individuals in Cleveland, Hensleigh said, he had a "generous aspect" to his personality. For Thanksgiving and Christmas holidays, Greene regularly purchased enough turkeys to hand out to the needy families in his neighborhood. He also subsidized the education of orphaned children.

"People in the Collinwood neighborhood spoke highly of him," said Hensleigh. "It's very unusual. You don't get that with most of these criminals. They usually just have that one facet – the violence, the megalomania, and the lust for power. Danny Greene had that, but he also had this man-of-the-people side."

Even Kovacic, the Cleveland police chief who had spent years chasing after Greene and his associates, recalled him fondly after his retirement. Greene reminded him of Marlon Brando in 'On the Waterfront,' Kovacic said.

"After you broke through that veneer that he put on, you could see he was such a convoluted character – he had so many sides, so many faces," he said. "Basically, he was a pretty decent guy who got caught up with living up to his reputation, to the image of being Danny Greene."

Irish actor Ray Stevenson, who portrayed Greene in the film, said it was Greene's passion that drew him to the role – not the obvious Irish-American aspects that linked the two.

"He had within him a kind of warrior's code. If you weren't in his line of work, he wasn't going to bother with you," Stevenson said. "But if you were one of the bad guys? Look out."

ABC News' acclaimed chief investigative correspondent Brian Ross was just a young reporter starting out with WKYC Channel 3 in the 1970s but earned himself a name in the industry when he started covering the Teamsters union. He interviewed Greene several times over the years, including after the bombing of Greene's Collinwood home in 1975.

"He was like a lot of big-time mobsters I had met," Ross recalled. "He had the air of someone who was gentlemanly and polite, but you knew there was this very dark side to him. In his dealings with me, he put on a veneer of charm and respectability – I guess that meant he cared about his image. It mattered to him how he was perceived."

Although "Kill the Irishman" is based on Greene's story and not a documentary, the film was still thirteen years in the making. According to author Rick Porrello, the historian behind the book that inspired the film, the release of the film was a "culmination" of years of waiting and wondering if the movie would ever be made.

"I see this becoming one of the top mob films of all time," Porrello said. "If that happens, it will cement Danny's place in history on a national and international level. It will take its place among the great mob stories of Al Capone and John Gotti, and the great organized-crime films like 'Goodfellas' and 'The Godfather' trilogy. At least, that's my hope."

A documentary called "Danny Greene: The Rise and Fall of the Irishman" was also released by filmmaker Tommy Reid, who produced "Kill the Irishman." Parts of the movie were filmed in Cleveland in 2008, and includes interviews with Kovacic, former Prosecutor Carmen Marino, Greene's former wife Nancy, and his daughter Sharon, as well as many others.

"It's such a rich part of Cleveland's history," said Reid, who had just graduated from Ohio State University when he bought an option for Porrello's book – before it was even published.

"We've had a lot of interest from people who remember Greene, but I also want to reach people who've never heard of him."

Greene's daughter Sharon was 21 when her father was killed – and had just celebrated her wedding two months earlier. Sharon had a "great life" growing up in Willoughby after her parents divorced, and had no idea about her dad's criminal enterprise.

"We didn't know what was going on," she said. "You didn't know what your father did back then. He was just this big guy to us."

Danny Kelly, Greene's oldest son, knew his dad was up to no good. Although he was only 17 when his father was killed, Kelly remembers his childhood with Greene vividly. Particularly, he recalls assisting his dad with tasks that included crawling underneath the car to look for explosives.

"He was Irish, Irish Catholic – he believed the man upstairs pulled the strings and that there was someplace to go after this," Kelly said. "Where he is today, he wouldn't trade places with either me or you here."

He also remembers his father as being both humorous and "truly intrepid."

"If you know somebody that has that charisma, that magnetism of the Irish personality, that was him," added Kelly. "He probably could have been governor or senator if he hadn't gone the other way."

FRANK LUCAS : THE KING OF NEW YORK

15

ANA BENSON

Many prominent crime figures rose to fame during the 1960s and 1970s in New York. The city itself was a fertile ground for drug dealers and mafia bosses who aimed to control poorer parts and neighborhoods. One of them was Frank Lucas who reached a legendary status when he reinvented the drug trade in the United States by smuggling the goods straight from the source. The drugs he sold were pure and he used the Vietnam War situation to his advantage.

Frank Lucas was an eccentric drug trafficker who led an intriguing life, but his kingdom didn't last for too long and he was soon placed behind the bars. He did change himself later in his life and became a law-abiding citizen. His wild adventures inspired the movie called *American Gangster* which was a huge box office success in 2007.

Early life

Frank Lucas was born on 9th September 1930 in La Grange, North Carolina. His parents were Mahalee and Fred Lucas who soon moved their family to Greensboro, North Carolina. It was a rural town struck by the depression which hit the United States during Frank Lucas' childhood. He worked on farms and did his best to earn some money for his family. But surviving the depression was tough and southern parts of the United States really did go through difficult times back then. The racism was prevalent and being African American was another obstacle while searching for a job.

But Lucas knew that he had younger brothers and sisters to take care of so he always managed to find some type of employment. He was often in trouble with the law which should have been a clear indicator of the career path he would soon take. Lucas was very outspoken about the event that made him become a crime figure. He was only six years old when five members of the infamous Ku Klux Klan appeared in the family's front yard. They were living in a small house back then and everyone was able to see what was happening. The scene itself must have looked frightening to young Lucas because the clansmen were dressed in white robes with the obligatory hoods on their heads.

They demanded to see Lucas' thirteen years old cousin who apparently glanced at a white woman earlier that day. It was not acceptable for them and they grouped around the boy, killing him right there in the yard. Even though Lucas told this tale numerous times, the police officers were never able to confirm the story. But having in mind the racial tensions which were apparent in the South back then, the chances are Lucas is telling the truth. This event made an impression on young Lucas. He grew up to be a troubled teen but he was mostly involved in petty crime. He was the oldest boy in the family and was aware of the role he had to play in bringing food to the table. When he was unemployed, he would steal fruits and vegetables. But he quickly realized that robbing people is more profitable. He would then wait in front of a local bar for drunk guests who were going home on foot and then empty their pockets of any valuables.

The law enforcement quickly realized what he was doing, so he aimed to find a real job. Lucas landed a position of a truck driver for one local company and he worked there for a year or so. However, he was attracted to his boss' daughter and started a relationship with her. When his boss found out, he got into an argument with Lucas that resulted in numerous death threats. But Lucas was quicker to react so he hit his employer with a pipe, stole all the money he could find in the office, and eventually set the entire building on fire. He was pretty certain that the police would knock on his door soon. Mahalee, Lucas' mother found out what he had done and urged his son to move out of the town. It was the only way to avoid the arrest and the trial. She told him to go to New York so he packed his bags and traveled to the Big Apple in search of a better future.

The talk of the New York City

Frank Lucas arrived in New York City during the summer of 1946. He was only sixteen years old and he settled down in Harlem. The neighborhood itself was an unsafe place back then and young Lucas would often encounter crime and illegal gambling right there on the streets. His family and friends told him to straighten up and find a respectable job, but it was obvious that old habits are hard to shake. Frank Lucas was aware of all the possibilities New York had to offer back then and since he was no stranger to crime, he knew what he had to do in order to earn money in the largest city in the world.

He wanted to get into illegal gambling and dealing drugs, but establishing himself first was more important. After all, he needed to get noticed by someone who was already well-known in the underground circles. Lucas did flee his hometown to avoid persecution so he was still feeling confident because of that move. Therefore, he made a decision to rob a bar. After he successfully pulled that off without getting caught or recognized, he moved on to a riskier job

– robbing a jewelry store. He had to fight the guard but Lucas did get away with plenty of diamonds. He then planned and executed a robbery of a very famous gambling club. Piles of money were at stake because the club was filled with high rollers. Frank Lucas got away with it once again.

Lucas was slowly finding his footing in the business of dealing drugs but he was not a big name yet. However, one drug deal will make him famous. A local criminal tried to cross Frank Lucas and he did not hesitate to teach him a lesson. Impressed by his work and boldness, Ellsworth Johnson, also known as Bumpy, wanted to meet Lucas. Bumpy was a kingpin of Harlem back in the days and he controlled all illegal gambling done in that part of New York. This was exactly what Lucas wanted because he needed someone to guide him. A well-known crime boss who knew how things worked in Harlem was the perfect teacher for Lucas. But there are two sides of the story here as well.

Lucas told the journalists that he was very close to Bumpy who eventually trusted him with some of the most important jobs he did back in the days. On the other hand, Bumpy claimed that Lucas was just a foot soldier who did not have much contact with him or the people who were running the gambling business. However, one thing is sure – Lucas benefited from this friendship because Bumpy taught him the basics of running a business. Lucas added his own flare to it which would help him move up the ranks quickly. Ellsworth Johnson died in 1968 and Harlem collapsed into a crime chaos because numerous fractions started fighting for the territory.

Rise to prominence

The 1960s and 1970s were an interesting time period in the history of the United States. Vietnam War was in full swing and the number of drug addicts that got hooked on the battlefield was growing steadily. There was also the free love movement that promoted peace and they were not strangers to opiates either. So the market was expanding each and every day. Selling drugs was a profitable business and everyone wanted a share of it.

After Johnson's death, Lucas focused on grabbing as much territory as he could in Harlem. It didn't go smoothly but he managed to control a midsized portion of the neighborhood which made him rise to the top alongside several other crime bosses. He wasn't interested in running illegal gambling only but wanted to broaden his business and make a fortune. Drug trafficking was on the rise in the city and the demand was high. Lucas did know a lot about it and believed he could become the biggest drug lord in the area. But this required a lot of planning.

Being one step ahead of everyone was important to Frank Lucas so he would often check into a hotel and spend weeks building strategies on his own. He would examine each possibility and find a proper response to every situation. Johnson did teach him a lot about the territory control but his death opened the door for the Italian Mafia, and now they had Harlem. Italian Mafia was into dealing heroin in the parts of New York which were once controlled by Johnson. Lucas understood that in order to drive them away from Harlem, he needed to create a brand new way of getting the drugs into the city. Drug dealers who were operating in Harlem bought the products directly from the Italians so Lucas' idea was based on cutting off the middle man and purchasing the drugs directly from the source.

Lucas understood the culture of the time and he analyzed the drug market thoroughly. He knew that the soldiers coming home from the front were heavily addicted to opiates because they had access to them in the military and that they would very likely continue their habits as soon as they land. Heroin was in demand but the supply was controlled by the Italians. Lucas would not profit a lot if he cooperated with them, so his plan was to get the drugs from the manufacturers. He knew where the drugs were made so Lucas decided to embark on his own little adventure. He hopped on a plane and headed out to

South-Eastern Asia, namely to Thailand where high-quality heroin was produced.

Frank Lucas did not know the language and he was clearly a foreigner but there was a large community of American citizens living in Bangkok at the time. It appears that Lucas was sure that he would connect with them quickly so he did not hesitate to start exploring the city on his own after checking into Dusit Thani Hotel. He did hear about *Jack's American Star Bar* so that was his next stop. The bar was frequented by African American soldiers who were stationed in the area and it was a place for rest and recuperation. Lucas wasn't aware of the fact that the place was run by Leslie Atkinson, also known as Ike, who was from North Carolina and was related to him by marriage. He trusted Ike right away and told him about his drug trafficking plans. Ike was well connected and knew many people from the area. Not to forget that he served addicted soldiers, as well as their drug dealers on a daily basis. Lucas would later say: "Ike knew everyone over there, every black guy in the Army, from the cooks on up."

Ike agreed to help Lucas make the deal with the heroin manufacturers, and the two decided to start working together. Lucas wanted to see the source of the drugs he was about to import into the United States, so he asked Ike to set up a meeting with their main drug connection. The two of them ended up traveling through the jungle in the unbearable Thailand weather, but they did eventually reach the poppy fields located on the border with Burma and Laos. The person who was running the business here was Luetchi Rubiwat, who was known in the underground circles as 007. It seemed like his setup was flawless because he had hundreds of acres under his control, as well as secret accommodations in the surrounding caves where the poppies were being processed. Lucas was astonished and amazed by Rubiwat's operation and he purchased 132 kilograms of heroin right away. Not to forget that the heroin was ten times cheaper than the one sold by Italian Mafia. So Lucas was about to make a huge profit back home.

However, getting the drugs out of Thailand and delivering them to the United States was a slight problem. But the two of them decided to use the war situation as best as they could in order to smuggle the heroin. It was the reason why Frank Lucas became a legendary figure – the drugs were stored in the coffins of dead American soldiers traveling back home. The legend says that the heroin packets were right next to the corpses, but Lucas never confirmed it. He told the press that he asked one carpenter from North Carolina to help him out and create false coffins that resembled the government issued ones. Each coffin had a double bottom which was used for storing the heroin without getting discovered by the authorities.

On the other hand, Ike claimed that the entire coffin story was completely false and that they used furniture with secret compartments filled with drugs. We might never know the truth, but one thing is for sure – Lucas was on a fast track to becoming the main drug lord of the New York City. He established his connections with the South East Asia and managed to surpass the Italians. Another interesting thing about Lucas' drug trafficking operation is the fact that he managed to create a team of soldiers who would work for him from Thailand. Those were servicemen who were friends of Ike, and Lucas paid them well. Of course, some high-ranking officials were not interested in this line of business but Lucas managed to pursue them to change their minds.

Once he got everything set up in South Eastern Asia, Lucas proceeded to create a group of trusted people who would handle the heroin once it arrived in the United States. He was very cautious when it came to selecting the people who would end up working for him. Lucas preferred his own blood relatives, or really good friends because he did not trust just anyone off the streets. Instead, he called up his five younger brothers and instructed them to move to New York. They proved themselves quickly and Lucas gave them their own portion of Harlem which was under their control. Recruiting his cousins and brothers gave Lucas security and ensured him that they would not try to steal from him.

But Frank Lucas applied some strange measures to make sure all of his employees were on the same page as him. For instance, he needed someone to mix and repack the drugs which arrived in New York, so he found several women who would do this in a highly guarded apartment. The women would sit around the table completely naked, wearing only surgical gloves. There was no way they could have taken even a little bit of heroin with them.

Lucas had another thing going for him and that was the quality of the product. Since he was the first link in the chain and he bought his heroin straight from the manufacturer, the drugs were purer than those offered by the Italian Mafia. If we consider the initial price which was lower than anything Italians could have offered, Lucas was about to make even more money than he imagined. He had an opportunity to cut the heroin and increase the volume of the product. As soon as the operation started, Frank Lucas became even more infamous on the streets of Harlem. If he was a violent man prior to the drug trafficking, now he was ready to hurt anyone who tried to endanger his business. And so the legend was created.

Even though this was never confirmed, Frank Lucas apparently earned a million every day. He would say so to his circle of friends, but it does seem unlikely from this point of view. We might never know the real numbers, but Frank Lucas was earning a lot of money on a weekly basis that allowed him to lead an expensive life and become one of the key players in New York's underground.

The lavish lifestyle

Since Lucas has the money, it was clear that the authorities will take a closer look at his estate sooner or later. Hiding the money was tough at first, but Lucas got a hold of it pretty quickly. He made connections in several banks all over New York City which were willing to exchange the bills he brought them for different ones. It was the perfect way to launder the drug money. He also discovered he could use the offshore banks in order to store the funds he couldn't launder. He had more than $54 million stashed at one point.

Lucas also invested in the real estate and had properties all over the United States, namely in Detroit, Los Angeles, and Miami. He owned houses, mansions, and office buildings. Not to forget an enormous ranch in North Carolina in which he invested a lot of money to keep it running. In order to create an appearance of a legit businessman, Lucas also started buying gas stations and making a small fortune by running a couple of dry cleaning places. When he was interviewed years later, he stated: "I wanted to be rich. I wanted to be Donald Trump rich, and so help me God, I made it."

But he wasn't all about the business and loved spending his time with the celebrities. He was a regular in some of the hottest nightclubs in New York back in the day and would dress up in his mink coats because they were a status symbol for him. He would often party with James Brown, Diana Ross, and Muhammad Ali. Lucas was married to Julianna Farrait who was a beauty queen from Puerto Rico. The two of them adored each other and did not shy away from buying insanely expensive presents. For instance, Julianna knew how much Lucas loved his coats so she found him a chinchilla coat and a hat made from the same material. She paid them somewhere around $60,000 which was basically change for Lucas back in the day.

On the other hand, Lucas would buy jewelry for Julianna and he once spent $140,000 for Van Cleef bracelets. But he was not flying under the radar anymore and the law enforcement was aware that something illegal was happening in his world. It was improbable that he was earning that amount of money for the work he was apparently doing. So they started digging deeper and uncovering various information that would eventually lead to the collapse of Frank Lucas' empire.

The legal troubles

The expansion of Frank Lucas' drug operation was enabled by the state of New York Police Department in the 1960s and 1970s. The city itself was a dangerous place to live in due to the number of corrupted departments that did nothing to protect the citizens. The police officers were easily bribed into silence which helped Lucas push his products on the streets of Harlem. However, New York Police Department's Special Investigations Unit was the worse because they were in charge of the whole city but did minimal work to stop the spreading of the crime wave.

The officers were aware of the drug dealers but refused to take them off the streets. Instead, they would extort the money from them in exchange for their freedom. Frank Lucas later claimed that he was arrested by one of the top ranking officers in that unit and that he simply led him to the police station, presented him with the evidence found in Lucas' car, and asked for money in order to be set free. Nobody even mentioned a possible trial or a jail time.

But there were other state-led agencies who knew what was going on in New York City and they wanted to clean up the place. Justice Department took it upon themselves to create a task force that will stop the organized crime in the largest city in the United States. They had a perfect man for the job and his name was Richard Roberts. He was a prosecutor so he knew quite a lot about the juridical system. Not to forget that Roberts was also a former marine who gave his best at every single assignment. Roberts could not be bribed and had a real moral compass. He became the leader of Special Narcotics Task Force at the beginning of the 1970s.

It was January of 1975 when an affluent neighborhood of Teaneck, New Jersey was swarmed with police who were zeroing in on Frank Lucas' estate. Julianna was at home and she was in a clear state of panic. She tried to get rid of the money which was stashed in the closets so she threw it out from the top floor window. The police saw the bags flying out and collected them as evidence later on. They also made a connection between Lucas and several offshore deposit boxes by uncovering keys hidden in the house. But there was no proof that could link Lucas with the drug trade at the heart of New York City. However, Richard Roberts did not want to give up and he continued digging.

The raid did lead to a dozen arrests and police were interrogating the suspects, hoping at least one of them would crack under pressure. And yes, they were right. One of Lucas' cousins started telling the whole story. He told the detectives everything he knew about the operation and listed names of those involved. Police continued with the arrests and up to forty people were charged with drug trafficking. The majority of them was somehow related to Frank Lucas. But the case against the kingpin was still pretty weak. Roberts knew that Lucas was the mastermind but pinning him down was near impossible. This didn't stop him from taking Lucas to a trial.

The entire case relied upon the drug-related deaths which were directly caused by Lucas' brand of heroin which was sometimes too pure for a human body to handle. Lucas called it the Blue Magic and as we have previously mentioned, it was very high-quality. The addicts who were used to heroin which was pushed by the Italians would often make a mistake in terms of dosage and an overdose was inevitable. The jury spent just a couple of hours on the final verdict and Frank Lucas was found guilty. He was sentenced to seventy years behind the bars. But Lucas wasn't wasting any time because he knew he was cornered. He started cooperating with the police and gave up all of his police connections, naming the corrupted cops, as well as Atkinson who was his right-hand man in Thailand.

Lucas reduced his sentence to a total of fifteen years just because he provided the detectives with the names of everyone involved in his drug operation. He was set free in 1981 but it was clear that he was not going to change his lifestyle. Frank Lucas was once again arrested in 1985. However, everything took a whole new turn when Roberts who persecuted Lucas back in the 1970s offered his help. He was an established defender and felt that Lucas needed a push in order to leave his criminal past behind. Even though Lucas was held on drug charges and faced at least fifteen years of jail time, Roberts managed to lower the sentence to seven years. Released in 1991, Lucas made a decision to change his life. He became really good friends with Roberts as well.

He is a different person now and started helping out his former neighborhood as much as he could. He was aware of the fact that his drug trafficking devastated Harlem and he is solely focused on rebuilding it. Frank Lucas is still alive and free but he is bound to a wheelchair due to a car accident. His crime escapades became famous all around the globe with the release of critically acclaimed Hollywood movie American Gangster, starring Denzel Washington.

PAUL CASTELLANO : MAFIA GODFATHER

SARAH THOMPSON

When one thinks of the Mafia, the mind goes to movies like the Godfather, almost on autopilot. The idea of the Mafia seems so far removed from real life, because of such sensationalized accounts. The Italian men in suites, the Don's granting favors, the schemes, lies, slander, and drama ... it all seems too fantastical to be real. Of course, even the Godfather was based off of a very real group of people who persist even to this day in modern iterations. While the American Mafia is no longer the reigning power in most cities, it was once one of the most powerful criminal organizations, with people mobster who existed at every level: from blue collar, to white collar. From working class to presidents of entire corporations.

The American Mafia is a criminal society that is highly organized. It can be otherwise known as the American-Italian Mafia, since so many of its members come from Italian immigrants, or American-Italian people. Most people, however, simply refer to it as the Mob for short. When one thinks of the 'Mob', they think of the forgiving Godfather, granting one wish on this, the day of his daughter's wedding. In 1985, the assassination of one American Mafia crime boss sparked years-long conflict between many of the crime families that dwell in New York. Paul Castellano, also known by his full name as Constantino Paul Castellano, is the namesake from which every "Big Paulie" character has been derived from.

Paul Castellano was born on a warm summer day. His mother, Concetta Castu, gave birth to her son Paul on June 26th of 1915. He was born with the full name of Constantino Paul Castellano - but it was a name that he hated. Castellano was known to always sign his name as simply "C. Paul Castellano". He was the youngest son of Concetta and Giuseppe Castellano, with an older sister by the name of Catherine. Castellano's father, Giuseppe, was a butcher. He was also a member of the Mangano crime family. As the son of a mobster, Castellano's life was already exposed to the life of a crime family. He was born and instilled with the specific brand of loyalty, values and sense of honor that was unique to members of the Mafia. Castellano's life, it seemed, would already be pointed in the direction of being a mobster from the moment he was born.

The Mangano family was what was known as the forerunner of the Gambino family. That is to say, the Mangano family consisted of the mobsters who would become part of the Gambino family when, eventually, the family switched hands and names. At the time, the Mangano crime family was one of "the Five Families" that ran the organized crime throughout New York City. Though the Mafia is nationwide, the Mangano family, as well as "the Five Families", operated strictly in New York. At the time, the other four families were the Maranzano, Profaci, Luciano and Gagliano family - all of which, including Mangano, would go through a change of hands, and a change of names. "The Five Families" were simply a handful of crime families - the Mafia operated all over the United States, from Dallas to Denver, from Pittsburgh to San Jose.

In the early 1900s, society didn't place the same stock and value in a good education as they do today. Born to a working class family, Castellano didn't succeed very far in his own education. Castellano went to school up until the eighth grade. After that, he decided to drop out and learn butchering, like his father. He also learned another trade, which was collecting numbers games receipts. Castellano, despite being born to a father who was involved with the Mafia, wasn't involved in his own criminal activities until later in life. In fact, it wasn't until Castellano turned nineteen did he first get arrested. A short escape from Brooklyn, Castellano was arrested while he was in Hartford, Connecticut. His first crime - or, rather, the first crime for which he was caught - was robbing a haberdasher (a store meant to sell accessories for men's clothing).

Castellano specific brand of Mafia loyalty lead to his refusal to name his accomplices in his haberdasher robbery. It was that very refusal that helped bolster his reputation as a young man who was loyal to his upbringing, and his eventual place in the Mob. Despite the loyalty, Castellano spent a three month stint in prison - but to Castellano, the reputation and protecting his accomplices within his found-family were worth the time spent.

In 1937, at the age of twenty-two, Paul Castellano married a woman by the name of Nina Manno. The couple would go on to have three sons, named Paul, Philip and Joseph, and one daughter by the name of Constance. Nina was Castellano's childhood sweetheart. While he married Nina, Castellano's sister, Catherine, went had previously married one of their cousins about ten years earlier - by the name of Carlo Gambino. It was Carlo Gambino who would go on -to be the future boss of the then-Mangano, soon-to-be Gambino family. After his marriage, things were slow for Castellano. His infamy was still years off. He spent most of his time involved in gambling rings, or bootlegging. He wasn't causing mischief or making trouble for the Mafia - but he wasn't gaining a reputation, either.

However, it wasn't too terribly long after Castellano's marriage to Nina that Castellano found his place among the crime family that his father had already been a long-standing part of. Several years later, after keeping his head down and working hard, Castellano was finally recognized as a full-fledged member of the Mafia. In the 1940s, during his mid-twenties, Castellano became an official member of the Mangano family. Under the watchful eye of the Mob boss Albert Anastasia, Castellano became what's known as a "capo".

A caporegime, more often shortened to capo, is a rank used in Mafia families. Castellano, as a made-member - rather, an official and fully initiated member - was given the title of capo. It's considered a ranking member of the Mafia, much like a senior sergeant in military terms. A capo is the head of his own branch, with members ranking under him. Castellano had earned a high-ranking title as a member of the Mangano clan, just two steps underneath his boss, Anastasia. As a Mob boss, Albert Anastasia was known as one of the most universally feared figures of the Mangano family. It was under Albert Anastasia that Castellano became capo - and it would be Castellano who would rule the Mangano family after Anastasia's death.

Life went on for Castellano, but his infamy wouldn't begin until 1957. On October 25th, in 1957, Anastasia was entering a barbershop on 58th Street and 7th avenue in midtown Manhattan. Anastasia had been left unprotected after his driver parked the car in an underground garage and took a walk. He was there in the barber's chair when two men rushed into the shop and began open firing. The inside of the barbershop was chaos, and in the rain of bullets, Anastasia had attempted to lunge for his attackers but had confused their reflections in the mirror for their real selves. In minutes, Anastasia had been killed.

Albert Anastasia's death left room for Carlo Gambino to rise to the level of Mafia Boss - thus, changing the Mangano family name to Gambino. Gambino was much different than his predecessor. His style of running the family was much more secretive. Where Anastasia was known to be volatile and dangerous, Gambino was much more low-key. While the Gambino switched hands, and names, Castellano was still operating in the Gambino family under his rank as a capo.

The same year that Anastasia was assassinated, Castellano attended the Apalachin Conference, in Apalachin, New York. The Apalachin Conference, or the Apalachin meeting, was a summit that gathered members of the American Mafia together. The summit was held at the home of renowned mobster Joseph Barbara - colloquially known as Joe the Barber. The meeting was held in order for different members of the surrounding Mafia families to get together and discuss important topics pertaining to the families as both individual entities, and as the American Mafia. Among the topics to be discussed, figuring out how to divide the illegal operations that had once been controlled by Albert Anastasia was among them.

An estimated one hundred Mafia family members attended the meeting, coming from both the United States, Cuba and as far away as Italy. When the expensive cars with plates from all over the United States began congregating, the local police enforcement in Apalachin began to grow suspicious. The Apalachin Conference was raided, and the members and leaders of the crime families from all over bolted from the house, some managing to escape into the woods surrounding Apalachin. Others were not so lucky.

Among the sixty-one mobsters that were arrested from the Apalachin Conference, Paul Castellano was among them. When put in front of a grand jury to answer questions about the meeting in question, Castellano refused to answer anything. His refusal and loyalty earned Castellano another stint in prison. Charged with contempt, Castellano spent a year in prison - and on January 13th, in 1960, Castellano was charged again, this time with conspiracy to withhold information. His sentence was five years, of which he only served eleven months. In November of 1960, Castellano had his conviction reversed by the Appeals Court.

Freedom from prison allowed Castellano to continue his life as a Mafia capo. Whereas other Mafia men were more prone to violence, Castellano was more of a businessman. He was not as violent as Anastasia, nor was he as quiet and secretive as Carlo Gambino. His forte was taking over businesses that lack legitimacy and turning them into profitable enterprises. His three sons also learned from Castellano's business ventures. Though, it was well known that it was Castellano's mafia ties that made his businesses a success. One of Castellano's businesses was Dial Poultry, something that he used his butcher's knowledge to help launch. Dial's Poultry was a poultry distribution company, and at its height, Dial supplied upwards of three hundred butchers in the New York City area, along with supermarkets like Waldbaum's. Despite the legitimacy of the business itself, Castellano was still a Mafia man, and intimidation was also part of the business scheme.

Castellano didn't just dabble in poultry, either. As he started his climb to power within the Gambino family, Castellano also worked in concrete for construction, raking in large amounts of money. Castellano's son, Philip Castellano, even served as the president of the Scara-Mix Concrete Corporation, which served the entirety of Staten Island when it came to concrete for their construction sites. Castellano's involvement with concrete businesses allowed him to control the Gambino family's interests in what was known as the Concrete Club. The Concrete Club was a gathering of different Mafia families that split up the revenue that was made from all of the New York developers. The American Mafia had their ties in all kinds of businesses, and concrete was one of the most lucrative. The Concrete Club even held permission over construction projects, and granted it to developers.

Despite being well-known as a businessman, Castellano was still a member of the Mafia, and his violence was not unheard of. In 1975, Castellano's only daughter, Constance, was dating a man by the name of Vito Borelli. Castellano had heard that Borelli had compared him to Frank Perdue, who was the owner of Perdue Farms. For whatever reason, Castellano viewed the comparison as an insult. Thus, Castellano had Borelli killed for the perceived slight. It was that same year, as well, that Castellano became acting pass for Gambino, who was growing older with the passing years.

Finally, on October 6th, in 1976, Carlo Gambino passed away. His death was not one fit for a Mobster. He didn't go out in a hail of bullets, but rather passed away, quietly, in his home. Gambino died of natural causes. Before his death, Gambino named Castellano as his successor to the Gambino crime family. In Mafia ranking, it's usually the underboss who succeeds as the Boss in the event of the Boss's death. However,

Gambino skipped over his second in command, Aniello Dellacroce, and named Castellano as the man who would take over the Gambino family. It was Gambino's understanding that Castellano would serve the family far better, since he had such a grasp on white collar crime, and an ability to produce money from his businesses and schemes.

On November 24th, 1976, Paul Castellano's ascension to Boss of the Gambino crime family was made official. Castellano had spent his entire life devoted to the Gambino family in all its iterations. He was now 61 years old when he became the official leader of the Gambino family. Dellacroce was kept as Castellano's underboss, and given the job of overseeing the Mafia activities of loansharking and extortion. Despite accepting the position, Dellacroce wasn't pleased with having been shirked for the succession of Carlo Gambino. Dellacroce, at the time of the announcement and Gambino's death, had been serving time in prison, and couldn't have possibly been able to contest what was happening on the outside. Castellano, effectively, stepped in and snatched Dellacroce's rightful place as Mafia boss out from under him. The move itself, and Castellano's deal to keep Dellacroce as his underboss caused a rift in the Gambino family that would never truly heal. The family split into two different factions - one for Castellano, and one for Dellacroce. Despite being under the same name of the Gambino family, the two groups rivaled.

Castellano began to rise to power in his place as the boss of the Gambino crime family. As the boss, Castellano began to show his violent hand more and more. In 1978, Castellano made several moves as the boss that reinforced the power that he now held. The first move was an order of assassination against a Gambino associate. The man killed was Nicholas Scibetta. Scibetta was a drug addict and alcoholic and was often the start of many fights. His behavior, to Castellano, was inexcusable, and he had to be dealt with.

The second move involved Castellano's alleged order of a hit against a Gambino capo, James Eppolito, and his son, a mobster by the name of James Eppolito, Jr. The senior Eppolito had complained to Castellano that another man, Anthony Gaggi, had been stepping into his territory, and wanted to kill him. Castellano granted Eppolito the right but warned Gaggi that the hit was coming - which caused Gaggi and another capo to kill both Eppolito, Sr and his son.

Castellano was more than just the businessman that had given him the advantage when it came to being named boss after Carlo Gambino's death. He was a mobster, through and through. In his first few years as head of the Gambino family, Castellano also initiated several alliances. One, with the Irish-American gang known as the Westies, due to the need for hit men that couldn't immediately be tied back to the Gambino family by local law enforcement. Another alliance was made due to Castellano's increasing need for a gunman, this time with the Cherry Hill Gambinos, who were heroin importers from New Jersey. These two alliances gave Castellano an endless supply of hitmen at his disposal.

At the age of 66, Castellano had been running the Gambino family for five years. In 1981, Paul Castellano was at the very height of his power, not to mention his wealth. He demonstrated both by building himself a mansion that had 17 rooms, standing on the ridgeline in Todt Hill in Staten Island. The house itself was designed so that it might resemble the White House in Washington D.C - a testament to both Castellano's immense wealth and power. The house itself was extravagant, with marble floors and gardens and swimming pools fit to host the Olympics. While the aging Castellano moved his wife, Nina, into the house with him, it was here that he began a love affair with his live-in maid, Gloria Olarte.

Castellano was no longer the man who would go out and do his business. In fact, once the mansion was built, Castellano became a misanthrope. He had no desire to venture out of his Todt Hill mansion and began to do so less, and less. Capos began traveling to the mansion to receive their orders and exchange information with their boss. The

Gambino family was already fractured from Castellano's ascension to power, along with the slight of Dellacroce having been passed up for succession as the leader. Castellano flaunting his power and wealth, and the elegance and expense of the mansion, caused even more of a rift among members of the Gambino family. They were envious and resentful of Castellano's lifestyle.

Those who supported Dellacroce were having trouble making money. Their support for Dellacroce had already turned them sour against Castellano, but having to watch him flaunt his money this way was enough to cause even more of a stir of hatred towards him. The capos working under Castellano were being forced to give him fifteen percent of their earnings - a raise up, from the typical ten percent that they had been previously been charged. Not only that, but Castellano was showing a touch of hypocrisy: accepting drug money from the Cherry Hill Gambinos, while banning other Gambino family members from running drug trafficking rings.

Perhaps, Castellano would have simply been allowed to live out his days as a successful, if not controversial, Mafia boss had it not been for John Gotti. John Gotti was part of the Gambino family and split onto the side of Dellacroce after Castellano's rise to power. Gotti stirred the pot when it came to the discontent that was running through the Gambino family. He fed it, nurtured it, and make sure that it continued to grow. Gotti was a capo, and he had his eyes on more than just causing trouble within the Gambino family. Despite all of his complaints and encouragement of discontent, Gotti was not seeking to overthrow Castellano - at least, not while Dellacroce was still alive.

Dellacroce would not leave Gotti free to overthrow Castellano for some years, yet. In the meantime, Castellano was facing a variety of legal troubles. In 1983, Castellano ordered a hit on one of his Mafia soldiers, Roy DeMeo. There was a trial coming up about a car theft, and Castellano was beginning to doubt DeMeo's loyalty, knowing well about the other man's unpredictable nature. The unrest in the Gambino family meant that Castellano could take no chances when it came to those who wanted to see him locked up, or dead.

Between 1983 and 1985, Castellano was eventually indicted on charges of federal racketeering, as well as the murders of Eppolito, Sr. and Jr. This took place after the FBI was granted permission to install covert listening devices in Castellano's extravagant mansion. The FBI was able to obtain more incriminating information about Castellano than they ever had been able to before, and lead to his arrest. Of course, with his connections, wealth, and power, Castellano was prompted released on a bail of two million dollars. Despite the seemingly never-ending legal trouble, Castellano was never placed in prison, which allowed him to be available for the upcoming trouble that was brewing within the Gambino family.

In 1985, Dellacroce finally passed away. Much like his Carlo Gambino before him, Dellacroce did not die a mobster's death. In fact, his cause of death was lung cancer, and he died quietly. The climate surrounding his death, however, was anything but quiet. From the time of Dellacroce's death, Paul Castellano had fourteen days left to live. The chain of events that transpired following Dellacroce's death would lead to Castellano's murder. After Dellacroce's death, Castellano did not attend the wake. Not only was this an act of blatant disrespect to Dellacroce's family, but it was also a slight to those who had split their affections for Dellacroce in the Gambino family. After all, Dellacroce had been Castellano's underboss. Refusing to attend the wake was a grievous insult.

With the position of underboss now open, Castellano decided to name Thomas Bilotti has his new right hand. Bilotti was loyal to Castellano, but he wasn't fit to be an underboss. Those in higher positions of power within the Mafia were expected to be able to act with a certain level of diplomacy. Bilotti wasn't this type of man. In fact, he was a loan shark and known to be extremely cutthroat. That wasn't all - Castellano had plans on having Gotti killed. All he needed was the proof. As it turns out, Gotti was doing what Castellano had forbidden the rest of the Gambino family to do, which was dealing with drug trafficking. Gotti was involved in narcotics trafficking, and Castellano needed government surveillance tapes to prove it. Once he had those in hand, he had plans on destroying the troublesome Gotti.

Castellano's plans were never to be played out. Two weeks after the death of his former underboss, on December 16th in 1985, Bilotti was driving Castellano to a meeting at a steakhouse in midtown Manhattan. Neither of them were aware that this trip out of his home, as infrequent as they were, would be the last that Castellano would ever make - and Bilotti as well, for that matter. A team had already been assembled, lying in wait. Gotti had decided that Castellano's time as the Don was over. Gotti had never seen Castellano as a fellow mobster. He didn't believe he had what it took - at the very least, he didn't have what it took to be head of the Gambino family. As Bilotti and Castellano made their way for the steakhouse, a team of hit men were waiting for them by the entrance and more waiting down the street. From his car across the street, Gotti watched.

Castellano was stepping out of Bilotti's car when two men bolted towards him, and opened fire. He was shot in the body, and in the head. He had no chance of survival. Bilotti was not spared in the undertaking. As he stepped from the driver's side, the men shot Bilotti as well. Surveying a job well done, Gotti drove to look at the bodies before he fled the scene - leaving Castellano dead, and ending his reign as Don of the Gambino crime family. Paul Castellano was 70 years old at the time of his death.

The death of Paul Castellano did not end his reign of power. In fact, his death was an unsanctioned one. Gotti had never received permission to take the hit out on Castellano, and his death infuriated the Don of the Genovese crime family, Vincent Gigante. The animosity between the Gambino family and the Genovese family lasted for years - to the point where Genovese had decided that Gotti would have to pay for his unsanctioned assassination of Castellano with his life. However, after a failed murder attempted with the use of a car bomb, Gotti and Gigante called a truce ... and the reign of Castellano officially ended. Despite Castellano's death causing unrest between the Gambino family and the other New York families, it was enough to bring the Gambino family back together from their previous schism of factions.

While Castellano's death signified the end of an era within the Gambino crime family, and organized crime in general, his legacy continues to remain. Though Castellano was simply one of many American Mafia crime bosses throughout the hundred or so years since his death, his legacy as head of the nation's largest crime families is still to be revered. Many have come after Castellano, but his name still inspires awe, perhaps fear, perhaps contempt, for those who still remember his stint as the Don. Films, books, and music still continue to reference Castellano, and explore his life and the impacts that he made to this day.

BUMPY JOHNSON : HARLEM GANGSTER

41

GARY JOHNSON

Ellsworth Raymond Johnson was called"Bumpy" by most. The nickname is the first of many mysteries surrounding the Harlem legend. Some claim he got the name as a child due to a bump on the back of his head. Others say it comes from his violent reputation and refers to him "bumping off people." Others still claim Johnson gave himself the name, referencing his ability to "bump people around" on the basketball court. Some have another nickname for Bumpy, to this day, they refer to him as the "Godfather of Harlem."

Bumpy Johnson was many things in his life, to many people. He was a stick up man, a burglar, a pimp, a drug dealer, a numbers runner, a bookmaker, a hood and a thug. He was also a husband and a father and a doting grandfather. He was the conduit between Harlem and the Genovese Crime Family. He was a respected friend of Lucky Luciano. He was a man of Harlem, giving to the needy, the hungry, and children. He was a staunch advocate for education, urging neighborhood children to stay in school and make something of themselves. He was a friend to the actors, starlets, and musicians who came from Harlem and who spent their late nights partying there. He spent time with the activists of the era, such as Malcolm X. He was a legend, all of Harlem knew him, many of Harlem still do. Yet, he never rose to the stature of fame that so many other gangsters of his era did. He was all these things, but he was also a private man, one who kept his secrets close, and to this day it is hard to find much information on him.

Johnson was born in Charleston, South Carolina on October 31, 1905 and spent most of his childhood there. He was not born to a poor family, instead his family was relatively middle class for the time period in the South. A smart boy, he had skipped two grades by the time he was 8 years of age. When Bumpy was only 10 years old his older brother, Willie, was accused of the murder of a white man. Bumpy's parents, fearing southern justice in the form of a lynch mob, sent Willie up north to live with family. Four years later Bumpy was showing all the signs of having a temper worse than his brother. Fearing Bumpy's insolence towards whites they sent their son off to live with his elder sister, Mabel, in Harlem.

While living with his sister Bumpy graduated from Brooklyn's Boy's High. He then went on to attend City college for a few semesters. While in college Bumpy set his aspirations high and studied pre-law. Finishing college wasn't in the cards though. Bumpy fell in with a rough and wild crowd. He left school and began a career in robbery and burglary. He found that he had quite the talent as a stick up man. His penchant for violence and other criminal activities caught the eye of Madame Stephanie St. Clair.

Stephanie St. Claire was one tough lady. Outside of Harlem she was known as "Queenie" but the people of Harlem referred to her as Madame St. Clair. St. Clair had been associated with the gang "The Forty Thieves" until she decided to branch off on her own. With 10,000 dollars of her own money St. Clair started her own numbers game, and took over Harlem with authority. The Madame dominated the numbers racket and much of the other criminal enterprises in Harlem. In fact, she ran one of the biggest and most profitable numbers operations in all of New York City. Bumpy began working for St. Clair as a leg breaker and enforcer. Of course, he was quite good at making sure the message was received when he paid someone a visit. He quickly became a trusted associate of her's, rising fast in the ranks. Eventually he became her principal lieutenant. Though she was 20 years older than Johnson, many believed the two were lovers for sometime.

Bumpy was no stranger to the wrong side of the law or prison. When he was released from Sing Sing in 1933 for an attempted grand larceny conviction he had already spent nearly half of his life behind bars. He wasn't even 30 years old yet. His proclivity for violence towards both inmates and guards caused Bumpy to be transferred frequently to different prisons. Thoroughout his criminal career he would spend time in Sing Sing, Alcatraz, Leavenworth, and Dannemora Prison. When he left Sing Sing he was broke and desperate for employment. He went back to working with St. Clair. And, it was upon that release that would begin to his ascent from criminal to legend and folk hero.

While Johnson was in prison Jewish mobster Dutch Schultz had moved in on the entire Harlem territory. Most of the Harlem bookmakers had turned their racket over willingly to Schultz, as they had no interest in a war. Madame St. Clair and a few others were still holding out. With Bumpy now out of prison and back at the Madame's side they waged a violent war against Schultz.

The war for control of Harlem was a bloody one. Over 40 people were murdered. Several kidnappings occurred. It was also a very lopsided war. Bumpy and St. Clair were ruthless and smart. However, Dutch Schultz had both connections in City Hall and had the backing of several Mafia allies. With control over police protection also in Dutch's back pocket Madame St. Claire, Bumpy and the other independent operators in Harem stood no chance. Dutch managed to gain and keep control over Harlem and its profitable numbers racket.

That should have been the end of it, and likely no one would remember Bumpy Johnson. Fortunately for Bumpy and St. Claire Dutch Schultz was a wild card with a terrible temper and poor impulse control. Dutch was federally indicted numerous times and becoming the prime target of the federal government and United States Attorney Thomas Dewey. Sensing weakness in Dutch's operations, and assuming a conviction was imminent, the Luciano and Genovese family began to move in on his territory, claiming they were only going to "watch over it" in case Schultz was sentenced to prison.

The relationship between Lucy Luciano and Dutch Schultz was one of mistrust. Luciano knew Schultz's reputation for violence and had no doubt that Dutch would try to take his territory back by force when an opportune moment presented itself. Not shockingly Luciano had little interest in giving Dutch back his very profitable territory. The opportunity never came. Schultz sought permission from the Mafia

Commission to assassinate U.S. Attorney Dewey. The commission refused to approve the move. They felt an assassination of a federal attorney would bring too much unwanted federal attention to the entire organization. When Schultz left the meeting in a violent rage Luciano saw his opportunity to cement his family's control over Dutch's former operations.

Luciano ordered a hit on Dutch Schultz and he was gunned down on October 23rd, 1935. The moment was sweet revenge for St. Clair and Bumpy. While Schultz lay dying in the hospital St. Clair sent him a telegram. It read simply, "As ye sow, so shall ye reap."

Bumpy's moment to ascend to legend would very soon come. In 1940 Johnson met with Lucky Luciano and made a deal with the Italian Mafia that would stand for the next 28 years. The deal gave St. Claire, Bumpy, and the other Harlem operators who had fought with them control over the Harlem numbers racket once again. Bumpy reused to negotiate on behalf of those Harlem operators who had handed their operations over willingly to Dutch, he had no interest in helping those who refused to fight for themselves. Bumpy's and the others operations would still participate in the Mafia's central gaming pool and Johnson became the conduit between Harlem and the Italian Mafia. In addition all of their operations were now under the protection of Luciano himself.

This bold move made Bumpy an instant folk hero in Harlem. No other black man had been able to step up and cut a deal with the Italians. That he had the courage to even attempt to meet with the Italians was stunning. That he met with the Italians and came away with a deal and their respect was the stuff of legends. It wasn't long after St. Claire and Bumpy regained control of the Harlem numbers racket that St. Claire decided to retire. She gave her entire operation to Bumpy. Bumpy Johnson was now the uncrowned crime boss of Harlem. From this point until his death no one could or would dare to run an illegal operation in Harlem without clearing it with Johnson first, and cutting him in, of course.

But, Bumpy Johnson didn't just negotiate a deal with Lucky Luciano. He built a relationship with the mob boss. The two often played chess together. At one point Johnson was sent to Dannemora, where Luciano was already serving time. The two were often seen talking, and in one instance Bumpy saved Luciano's life, preventing him from being shanked. Two years before Luciano died in 1962 e sent a wooden hand carved chess set to Johnson's wife. Many would later claim that Luciano and Johnson were not friends, but when you talk to those that were close to either there is much evidence they had a mutual like and respect for each other

Just because Bumpy had a good relationship with the Italians didn't mean he laid down for them. His primary concern wasn't pleasing the mafia, but instead looking out for the people of Harlem. In one instance some Italians began to move in on one of Bumpy's bankers. In response Bumpy called a meeting of all the bankers, controllers, and runners of Harlem. What was said specifically in the meeting is unknown, but it lasted 3 hours. The next day the result of the meeting became clear. More than half the runners for the Italians called in sick. Those that did come to work seemed to be working at a slower than leisurely pace. The receipts for that day dropped drastically and the point was made to the Italians. Luciano set a meeting up with Bumpy in Luciano's suite in the Waldorf Astoria. The two men met and talked and the issue was settled and Bumpy's people went back to work.

In another incident members of the Italian crew came into Harris's Bar in Harlem and dragged out one of the customers. No one in the bar dared make a move to stop them, as interfering in mob business rarely ended well. Someone did run to tell Bumpy, and when he couldn't be found he was phoned at his house. After getting all the information he could, Bumpy jumped in to his car and drove off. An hour later the kidnapped man was free and strolling back into the bar he had been dragged from earlier. Somehow, even though the man had made some kind of mistake with the mob, Bumpy was able to use his pull to get him off. That was Bumpy, he was able to his power and the respect he had earned from the mob. This was just one more thing that made him someone not to be underestimated or to be messed with.

Known for being a dapper dresser, Bumpy was often seen out and about in a black suit, complete with a tie and a black Fedora. Though he was a smaller man, standing about 5'8" and weighing around only 170 pounds Bumpy Johnson was feared for a reason. He was almost always armed. He carried both a knife and a gun on him at almost all times. His temper and penchant for violence was well known and well documented. During one of his many prison stays Johnson spent 3 years in solitary confinement for his violent behavior against other inmates and even the guards.

Another well shared story regales the day Bumpy beat a man in a night club. The man was badly injured and taken to the hospital. That should have been the ed of it. Hours later, however, Bumpy was told the man intended to rat him out to the authorities. Enraged, Bumpy rushed to the hospital and beat the man again, while he was on the operating table, while shocked Doctors and nurses watched.

Though he was never arrested for killing anyone, no one doubts that Bumpy was capable of murder, or that he may have been behind more than a few. He didn't shy away from violence, nor did it effect him. While waiting for his table at a restaurant Bumpy attacked a rival, almost gouging out one of his eyes and badly beating him. After beating the man witnesses claim Bumpy calmly stood up, straightened his tie, and inquired if his table was ready. Bumpy is said to have told those with him he suddenly was in the mood for spaghetti and meatballs. When necessary the man could have ice in his veins.

Bumpy often told people he was a barber. He is even listed on the 1940 United States Census as one. His granddaughter, Margaret, has joked that he was in fact quite skilled with a straight razor. Of course he wasn't giving haircuts. In the early 1930s Bumpy went after Ulysses Rollins, an enemy enforcer, with a switchblade. He slashed the man over 30 times. Rollins was lucky to survive.

Bumpy wasn't just unafraid of getting violent to handle things, he also had little fear of death or being harmed. In one incident a man cut Bumpy off while he was driving his Cadillac, then stopped his vehicle, jumped out of his car and began firing at Johnson. Unarmed at the moment, an unphased and unafraid Bumpy jumped out of his vehicle and began running at the man shooting at him. As the bullets flew past him Bumpy kept running towards the man. Likely shocked, and a little scared, the man stopped firing and ran back to his car, getting in and driving off before a very angry Johnson could reach him. After this incident some would say Bumpy scared people so much they couldn't even shoot straight when facing him.

To many, including Bumpy himself possibly, the man must have seemed immortal. Many expected him to meet a violent end. It wasn't for lack of attempts. Over his lifetime he had been shot, stabbed, and assaulted. But, Bumpy always survived. While other mobsters, gangsters, and mafia men met untimely ends Bumpy Johnson wouldn't die and he wouldn't stay down.

In 1948 Bumpy had just finished yet another prison stint. This time he had served 10 years at Dannemora in upstate New York. Bumpy walked into a diner on Seventh Avenue and saw Mayme Hatcher sitting alone and eating. While she ignored him, he was intrigued and sat down at her table. The two talked for a while, and Mayme was so taken with Bumpy they left the restaurant together and went to the movies. The two were together from that point on. A month later Bumpy proposed. The two were on a drive when he looked at Mayme and told her "You and I ought to get married". She simply responded, "is that so?" Two months later they were married in a small civil ceremony. Meeting in April and marrying in October, the two would be together for the rest of Bumpy's life and Mayme would speak lovingly of Bumpy until she died in her early 90s.

Their life was one of luxury. Bumpy's criminal enterprises provided them with more than enough money. They lived in spacious, beautiful apartments. They traveled to Europe. Bumpy bought Mayme several furs, she could have anything her heart desired. Many women were jealous, many women tried to steal him away. But, Mayme would always be Bumpy's girls.

The couple raised their two daughters together, both girls were from previous relationships. Ruthie was Mayme's daughter but Bumpy loved her as his own. Mayme in turn loved Elease, Bumpy's daughter as her own. The two also raised their granddaughter, Margaret, as their own. Bumpy doted on all three girls. The girls had lavish birthday parties complete with pony rides. There was nothing he wouldl deny them. They often went to Aqueduct and Belmont to place bets on the horses. Bumpy even had chauffeur driven limousines take the girls to private school.

It was 3 years after Bumpy and Mayme married that Bumpy had his closest brush with death. Bumpy was at an after hours club on West 122nd, The Vets Club. It was close to 5:30 a.m. when a drunken Robert (Hawk) Hawkins strolled up to the bar. Hawk was a wannabe pimp, a young loud gambler from North Carolina. He was looking to make a name for himself, though many believe he didn't immediately realize it was Bumpy standing at the bar. Bumpy was near Hawk and overheard him speaking vulgarly in the presence of a friend's girl and a few other women. Bumpy scolded Hawk when he cursed in front of the women at the bar. In spite of his bad ass reputation, Bumpy abhorred cursing or smoking in front of women.

The two exchanged words and Hawk left drunk, embarrassed, and angry. He returned an hour later, having borrowed a revolver from a friend. A very quick struggle ensued. Bumpy managed to hit Hawk with a potted plant as Hawk fired off one shot at him. The bullet meant for his head hit Bumpy in the chest and bumpy fell to the ground. For a moment Hawk likely though he had killed the legend. But, Bumpy opened his eyes and Hawk ran from the bar. Bumpy stood slowly. The owner of the bar and a bartender drove Bumpy to Sydenham Hospital on Manhattan Avenue.

The bullet struck less than an inch away from Bumpy's heart, and surgery took 6 hours. By the time Mayme Johnson made it to the hospital many of Bumpy's friends and associates were also there. The police were there too, desperately trying to get Bumpy to tell them who had shot them before he possibly slipped away for good. Mayme shooed the police away and prayed for her husband. The doctors were uncertain Bumpy would survive. Bumpy was in a coma for 5 days. During that time the nuns of the neighborhood church lit candles for his recovery, indeed all of Harlem waited with baited breath to see if the Godfather would pull through. There was an endless procession of visitors to the hospital. Many nurses would later tell of how often and well they were slipped cash by the gangsters and mafia that came to visit, they all wanted to see Bumpy well taken care of. When he did at last open his eyes he gave his wife a weak smile, and then began humming "It Had to be You." Yes, Bumpy had survived.

Bumpy Johnson wasn't just a violent gangster. He was a complex character, one that was loved just as much as he was feared. He may have been a "tough guy" but he was also well known by Harlemites for his generosity. Some referred to him as the "Robin Hood of Harlem." He loved to help the poor in the community and was known for his gifts and the cash he freely gave to them. During the depression he sponsored neighborhood bread lines. He gave turkeys to the poor in Harlem at Thanksgiving. He also sponsored many neighborhood block parties. He would pay the rent of those about to be evicted. If ever there was a need Bumpy was there to help. He may have taken from the community but he never hesitated to give back to it.

It was children that held a special spot in Bumpy's heart and he showed it in his generosity. Every Christmas Bumpy spent thousands of dollars on presents for the children of the neighborhood. He would help with school clothes, books,money for shoes, whatever the children of Harlem needed. Often, he would be spotting strolling down Lennox Avenue deliberately and noisily jingling the change in his pocket. Behind him a small horde of children would follow. Bumpy would walk into the ice cream shop and order a dish of vanilla ice cream for himself, and then grandly gesture to the kids behind him, "Give them whatever they want" he would state.

Bump's generosity wasn't just in nature. It was also a good business decision made by a very smart man. The good will his many good acts bought him made it easier for others to turn a blind eye to his criminal activities. Bumpy was a giving man who loved children and took care of the poor. He refused to curse or smoke in the presence of women he didn't know. He was also a mobster, a pimp, a robber, and the king of all of Harlem's illegal enterprises. It was his intelligence and fearlessness that made those two personas work so well together.

During his total 26 years in prison Bumpy furthered his education. He loved reading, and was known to read and quote literature often. Bumpy also found an interest in poetry. He even wrote some poetry of his own, pieces of which were later published during the Harlem Renaissance. Bumpy was a skilled chess player. He loved literature and it is said his library at his home was more than extensive. The Harlem mobster could even read Latin.

Later in life Bumpy did attempt to go legit, or at least he steered a portion of his empire legitimate. He became the proprietor of an insect extermination company based in Manhattan. However, in 1952 Bumpy was brought up on federal charges of conspiracy to sell heroin. Though he was convicted, Bumpy maintained his innocence, claiming he was framed. Johnson was sentenced to 15 years and sent to Alcatraz. Even in Alcatraz Bumpy found a way to further his legendary status. A well-believed rumor has Bumpy helping 3 inmates escape, arranging for a boat to pick them up. This escape was the first, and only successful escape from Alcatraz, and of course Bumpy had a hand in it. Johnson, himself, stayed put and was released from Alcatraz in 1963.

Arrested more than 40 times Bumpy was no stranger to the law. He wasn't afraid of the law either. In 1965 Bumpy Johnson staged a sit-down strike at a police station to protest what he felt was excessive surveillance of himself and his associates. Refusing to leave the police station he ended up being arrested. He was brought before a judge on charges of refusal to leave a police station. The judge acquitted him.

Bumpy wasn't just respected and even loved by the people of Harlem. He also rubbed elbows with many celebrities. Johnson was known to hang out with Bill "Bojangles" Robinson and Billie Holiday. Not only was he friendly with the great Lena Horne, many believed he had a brief fling with her. He was also a good friend of Sugar Ray Robinson. He was the godfather of Sydney Poitier's eldest daughter. Bumpy interacted with just about anyone who was anyone from Harlem.

He was also a good friend, supporter, and protector of many black activists. He and Paul Robeson were good friends. It was Bumpy and his associates who went and rescued Paul from the violent riots in Peekskill. Bumpy also offered both protection and other services to Malcolm X just days before his assassination. Bumpy felt strongly that Malcolm should respond with violence to the threats against him. Malcolm declined, stating he didn't want to see "black folks killing black people." Days later Malcolm was dead, assassinated. Bumpy was said to have been quite upset that Malcolm didn't take him up on his offer of protection, feeling he could have saved him.

On July 7, 1968 after eating dinner with Mayme the two sat down to watch The Laurence Welk show. Bumpy got up and said he was heading to bed. A few moments later he changed his mind deciding to go out instead. He said good night to his wife and left with his childhood friend Junie Bryd. He took $500 cash with him. He and Junie went to a card game. After Bumpy had lost almost all of the money he brought with him he left the game alone. It was around 2 a.m. when Bumpy Johnson walked in to Wells Restaurant in Harlem. He ordered his usual, a fried chicken leg, hominy grits, and coffee. The waitress had just brought his food and he had just begun to eat when Bumpy fell to the floor, shaking and clutching his chest. A nurse, who happened to be there eating rushed to try to help. Finley Hoskins, a long time friend of Johnson, was there, and rushed to Bumpy's side as well. Someone ran from the restaurant to get Junie Bryd, who was at the Rhythm club down the street. Bumpy was alive, but not conscious, when Junie got there. Cradling Bumpy in his arms, Bryd watched as his good friend opened his eyes for a moment and smiled. And then Harlem's Godfather died. It wasn't bullets or a knife or at the hand of a rival that Bumpy Johnson left this world. Instead, he died of a heart attack in the presence of two of his closest childhood friends.

Bumpy Johnson's death and funeral was headline news. The headline of *Amsterdam News read,* "Bumpys Death Marks End of Era." The church was full. So full, that the crowd spilled out onto the street for several blocks. It seemed that everyone in Harlem was in attendance. Bumpy had touched that many lives.

Before her death in 2009 Mayme Johnson was vocal about her husband's legacy. She wrote her own book, prompted in large part, by the portrayal of her husband in the movie "American Gangster." Frank Lucas claims that Bumpy was a mentor to him and that he became Johnson's second in command. Lucas also claimed that Bumpy died in his arms, yet it is well known he didn't. In fact, Mayme asserts that not only did Bumpy not trust or like Frank Lucas, but that he was no where near the restaurant where Bumpy died on the night of his death. Mayme further asserts Lucas wasn't even at Bumpy's funeral. She also said that while Frank Lucas may have driven Bumpy on occasion there was no way he was her husband's driver. Bumpy preferred to drive himself. In addition he wasn't out of prison for 15 years so Lucas's claim he was his driver for 15 years is impossible. Mayme asserts that Frank Lucas is a liar, and that Bumpy knew that, referring to him as such when he was alive. Frank Lucas may have been in Bumpy's life but he was not part of his inner circle. Instead, according to his wife, he was a wannabe and a hanger on, who assumed everyone who knew better was likely dead.

"American Gangster" wasn't the first time Bumpy was portrayed in a mainstream movie or media. He may not be nearly as well known as many gangsters of his time but he still popped up often in movies and television. He is the inspiration for the character, Bumpy Jonas in "Shaft." In "The Cotton Club" the great Laurence Fishburne plays a character based off Johnson, Bumpy Rhodes. The movie "Hoodlum" portrays the struggle for control of Harlem between St. Claire, Bumpy, and Dutch Schultz. Once again Bumpy is played by Fishburne. Mayme Johnson has said that Hoodlum didn't get everything right. However, unlike "American Gangster" she felt that the inaccuracies were accidental, and they didn't bother her. She notoriously proclaimed she would never see "American Gangster" because if Lucas had lied about his relationship with her husband he had likely lied about everything else in the movie as well.

Bumpy Johnson was a private man. Even though his legend lives on there is little on paper about him. His own granddaughter turned to a genealogy website in hopes of finding more information about the man who raised her and loved her. Most of his close associates are dead and gone. His wife and daughter are both now dead too. He was respected, revered, and feared. When he was alive he owned Harlem. Many of the long time residents of Harlem knew of him, and there are many personal stories and legends about the man. Yet, once he was gone his reputation never rose to the status of many of the mobsters almost everyone knows by name. But, Bumpy was a private man, and likely he would have wanted it that way.

ALBERT ANASTASIA : THE GREATEST MOBSTER

AMY DELANEY

Albert Anastasia

"Anastasia loved to look his victim's in the eyes while killing them slowly just to show his ruthlessness. Anastasia would kill anybody, he would kill police, judges, prosecutors, politicians, mayors, governors, even federal agents in a heartbeat, which he did, he did not care who he killed, he just loved to kill. Nobody got on the wrong side of Albert Anastasia and got away with it."[1]

The Early Years

Albert Anastasia was born Umberto Anastasio in Calabria, Italy, on February 26th, 1902 to Raffaelo Anastasio and Louisa Nomina de Filippi.

He became used to death at an early age – although he had 11 siblings (8 brothers and 3 sisters), three of them died in childhood. His father, Raffaelo, died when Albert was just 10 years old.[2]

With his railroad worker father dead, money was tight, so Albert left school when he was 12 to find work and help support his family.[3]

He started work on a steamship as a deckhand, but life was hard. He was among men who were strong, and tough, and the work was extremely physical, especially for a young boy. But Albert stuck it out, and when he was 15 he said goodbye to Italy for good.

New York

It was 1917, and Albert, along with three of his brothers – Anthony, Joseph, and Gerardo - arrived in America on board a freighter. They entered illegally, having jumped ship, and managed to integrate themselves into the longshore gangs which worked the docks.

Albert was quiet – not from shyness or unsociability – but because, having left school at a young age neither his English nor his Italian was fluent.[4]

When he arrived he was penniless, without even a pair of shoes to his name and no education. But what he lacked in brains, he made up for with sheer strength, and those in charge of hiring and firing weren't interested in a worker's IQ.

He worked hard. The pay wasn't great but there were some perks to being a longshoreman – bosses would turn a blind eye to the stealing which went on among the workers, and there were often fights about which team got to unload the most lucrative cargo. Albert was never shy about using his fists to defend his team's privileges.

He began to earn a reputation and was known as *'terremoto'*, the Italian for earthquake. A nickname that was well deserved.

'That's exactly what he was…you never could tell…something…who knew…would set him off'[5]

His First Arrest

On March 17th, 1921, Albert Anastasia was arrested for the murder of fellow longshoreman, Joe Torino. A dispute had broken out over who had the 'rights' to pilfering the worthwhile cargo. Albert was angry – Joe Torino appeared to be making sure his men got to the good stuff first, and Albert felt that he, and his men, were missing out and deserved more.

A fight ensued. Both men were tough and neither one of them would acquiesce. Things got ugly. Albert got the upper hand and proceeded to stab and then strangle Joe Torino to death. There was no attempt to hide his actions, and he had no regard for the people standing around, watching in horror the scene which unfolded before them. When interviewed, the onlookers described Albert as appearing to take pleasure in the killing.[6]

"Neither man backed down. Tempers flared. 'They started fighting and Anastasia lost his temper.' The 18-year-old stabbed Torino repeatedly. 'What everyone talked about was the look on his face. I mean, it was maniacal, he loved every minute of it.'"[7]

Albert was arrested, and in July of that year he was convicted and sentenced to death. He was sent to the notorious Sing Sing prison in Ossining, New York, where he was kept in what was known as a 'death-cell' to await execution by electric chair.

It was around this time that Albert changed his name from Umberto Anastasio to Albert Anastasia, reportedly to protect his family from the shame of his arrest, but Albert had already set his sights on a life of crime and using variants of a name was a tactic used by gangsters and criminals to cause a headache for law enforcement.[8]

While working as a longshoreman, prior to his arrest, Albert had already come to the attention of the mafia. Each morning, as the men vied for work on the docks, a rep from the mafia called the Loading Boss would scan the throngs of workers. Any man who was signalled by the Loading Boss would have to surrender part of his salary to the mob.[9] Albert was one of those men.

Now, incarcerated at Sing Sing prison and waiting for his execution date, Albert found himself once again having to rely on his fists to gain respect. A fight broke out as the inmates queued for food, and the prison barber noticed how Albert held his own.

Jimmy DeStefano, or Jimmy the Shiv, was a mobster who was serving time in Sing Sing, and he considered himself as something of a 'talent scout' for the mafia. When he saw how Albert conducted himself in prison, he brought the young Italian's name to the attention of a mobster who went by the name of Lucky Luciano.

"He said this is the toughest kid I have ever seen in my life. This kid's got nerves of steel, he would kill you in a heartbeat, this is the kind of guy you could use."

Albert fell under the protection of the mob.

A lawyer acting for Albert won a re-trial. But before a new trial could be set, three of the witnesses died, and a fourth simply vanished. The mob had done its job, and Albert's murder charge was dropped.

"And from that, Albert learned the most important lesson of all...if you've got witnesses, you kill them."[10]

By spring 1922, he was free to go.

Mafia Life

Albert returned to working on the docks, but he had gained notoriety in the underworld, and when he returned to work it was as a mafia enforcer. Now he was the one who was collecting a chunk of the men's wages. He was also charged with keeping order on the docks, and he did so with violence.

This work brought him into contact with gangsters, a world he had set his sights on when he first left Italy at the age of 15. His circle of 'friends' included the likes of Frank Costello and Lucky Luciano, the young mobster who had first heard of Albert from Jimmy the Shiv.

Albert was ambitious, and would not shy away from using whatever means necessary to get ahead on the mafia ladder.

In 1920 prohibition came into force, and was a golden opportunity for organized crime. Prior to that, their job was mostly about violence and murder, but with the ban on alcohol, mobsters really came into their own.

"Prohibition was the greatest thing that ever happened to organized crime. Prior to the passage of prohibition, organized crime groups were essentially thugs."

While 'old mobsters' were only interested in rival gangs, Lucky Luciano saw an opportunity for making money. Albert was only too happy to stand behind him.

"Anastasia thought if he hitched himself to Luciano's coat tails, that he was going to go someplace too. He told Luciano that he would kill whoever he needed to have killed."[11]

Fight for Power

In 1910 the head of the underworld, Giuseppe Morello, had been imprisoned, leaving organized crime without a leader. Salvatore D'Aquila took over, but when Morello was granted an early release

D'Aquila was concerned that he would lose his position as head of the underworld. A meeting was called, from which Morello and his supporters walked out, prompting D'Aquila to declare a state of war among the rival factions, causing the former boss to go into hiding to escape certain death from D'Aquila's supporters.

Newspaper reports suggest that Albert was involved in this bloody feud, although no official records support this. Either way, he wasn't involved for long because, in June 1923, he was imprisoned for two years at Blackwell's Island Penitentiary for being in possession of a gun. The feud continued without him, and by the time he was released, although D'Aquila was technically still the boss, a new power was ruling the city – Giuseppe Masseria, one of Morello's staunch supporters.

Upon his release, Albert resumed his criminal dealings at the docks – by this time his extortion had extended to both the workers and their employers. His association with Lucky Luciano and other gangsters continued, and at first, they sided with Masseria. However, in April 1931, Luciano ordered a hit on the boss.[12]

On April 15th, 1931, Luciano asked Giuseppe Masseria to meet him at his favorite haunt on Coney Island for lunch. After a heavy meal, the two men began to play cards.

"At one point Luciano said 'excuse me, I have to go to the bathroom'. The door swung shut behind Luciano. Masseria was alone. Enter Albert Anastasia and three others. Joe Masseria went down in a hail of bullets, his clothes soaked with food, and blood. 'What he has in his hand is the ace of spades and that becomes the sinister card, the card indicating death, the card indicating bad luck for any individual in organized crime.'"[13]

The mafia had a new boss, Salvatore Maranzano, who declared himself leader when he learned of Masseria's death, but members of the underworld had been becoming more and more angry with Masseria's interference. Five months later, Maranzano was executed.

A new system came into force, under the direction of Lucky Luciano. Rather than having one boss overseeing every mob family, a commission of several leaders was formed, who would be responsible for dealing with disputes between families.[14]

Murder Inc.

In 1932 and 1933 Albert Anastasia was charged with two separate murders. Both cases were dismissed when no witnesses could be found for either case. During this time, an organization called Murder Inc. had been formed, and Luciano offered Anastasia leadership of the group. It was a 'murder for hire' enforcement group, formed to carry out hits on those with a price on their heads.[15]

In the meantime, Luciano was shaking up the mafia. The inter-fighting had to stop, and he laid out a set of rules which each member had to abide by. One of those rules was that civilians and politicians were off limits, a rule imposed not for his sense of honor, but because such a killing would bring too much attention to the mob. Each city would now be presided over by one family, with New York being the exception – there were five mafia families in New York, each running a different facet of crime. Luciano was one, along with Joseph Bonanno, Tommy Gagliano, Joe Profaci, and Vincent Mangano. It was as Mangano's underboss that Anastasia worked.

It wasn't a happy alliance.

"Mangano became aware of the fact that Albert had connections. Luciano liked him, Frank Costello liked him, and they tended to bypass Vincent Mangano in talking to Albert."

As a collective, the five families, along with the other mob bosses from across the country were known as 'The Commission', and any murders carried out by the mafia had to be authorized by them and carried out by Murder Inc. Reckless murders were a thing of the past.[16]

Murder Inc. carried out their business under the guise of Midnight Rose's candy store in Brooklyn, and according to Albert's business card he was a sales rep for a mattress company. But Murder Inc. was a highly effective setup.

"These guys had a reputation as being very effective at killing...leaving no trace, leaving no clues. It's estimated that as many as maybe a thousand hits, not only New York but all over the country. Unlike a lot of gang bosses who killed as a result of doing business...Anastasia liked to kill people, he liked to see people get killed, he liked to participate in the killings."[17]

Although Murder Inc. had stayed under the radar of the police, their death toll had not. There was a rise in the number of murders across the country, with the most prevalent being in Brooklyn. The police's investigations into the mob intensified.[18]

On August 2nd, 1933, Albert took out a laundryman when he heard on the grapevine that the man was complaining about paying the mob. A witness identified Albert as the killer of Joe Santano but changed his story after being scared off testifying. Once again, Albert Anastasia got away with murder.

Thomas Dewey

Up until the mid-1930s, the mafia had had a relatively easy ride as far as law enforcement went. But in 1935 Thomas Dewey, the special prosecutor in New York declared war on organized crime. He was determined to crack down on organized crime and made no secret of the fact. Dewey was not interested in starting small – top of his most wanted list was none other than Lucky Luciano. After all, he had his pick of crimes to pin on the mob, including racketeering, organized prostitution, and, of course, murder.

But as determined as Dewey was, he just could not get the evidence he needed to put Luciano away for his many brutal crimes. The mobster was an expert in his field and left nothing with which to pin the crimes on him. All the prosecutor could manage to convict him of was organized prostitution. But it was better than nothing, and at least it got one mafia leader off the streets.

In 1936, the case came to trial.

"Boom! Conviction. 30 years in prison. Shocked organized crime to its foundations. Oh, my God, you got Luciano…who's safe after that?"[19]

Elsa

The following year, Albert got married to Elsa Barnesi, a 19-year-old Canadian woman.[20] Together they had four children – two boys and two girls. To all intents and purposes, he was a respectable family man, selling mattresses and, allegedly, running a dress factory. But behind the scenes, he very much lived up to the name he was given while slaughtering people in the name of murder inc., – The Lord High Executioner. Anastasia was notorious, and yet his wife and the mother of his four children claimed to know nothing of his criminal activities. However, this was hard to believe.

"I don't believe that anybody could live with anybody over a period of years, raise children with that person, and not know they were mobsters. I'm quite sure she did. But what he did in business and what he did at home were two completely different things."

He kept up the façade very well – attending church regularly, abstaining from alcohol, and returning home to his wife and children after work every night.

But nobody could be that naïve.

Lepke Buchalter

With Luciano safely behind bars, Thomas Dewey, the special prosecutor who had his sights set on the mob, turned his attention to Lepke Buchalter, Albert's partner in Murder Inc.

He wanted Buchalter on drugs charges, and a large reward was offered for information leading to his arrest. The police searched far and wide for the Murder Inc. hitman but didn't think to look in the one place he was hiding – Brooklyn.

Albert kept Lepke hidden, and, as he had learned early on in his mobster career, he went in search of the witnesses who could put Lepke away. One by one the witnesses began turning up dead and still more disappeared. One remained, however, and Albert set about taking him out.

A discussion between Albert and the two hitmen he hired to murder Morris Diamond was overheard by another member of Murder Inc., Abe Reles.

In May 1939, Morris Diamond joined the other witnesses against Lepke when he was shot and killed on his way to work. With no witnesses against Lepke, Dewey forged ahead. But with the search for Lepke came undue attention on the rest of organized crime, and the gangsters began to feel uncomfortable. Under the scrutiny of Dewey and the FBI, their activities were stilted.

"The mob realized, so long as Buchalter is on the lam, we're under terrible pressure. They're harassing all our operations, down on the street level we can't breathe...we're being suffocated. Is he worth it? No."

The rest of the mafia tried to force Lepke to give himself up, for the sake of the mob. His one ally was his old friend, Albert Anastasia, who encouraged him to stay on the run. But that put Albert in the line of fire – he was going against the mob by telling Lepke not to give up. He was caught between a rock and a hard place. Albert had to make a decision – stick with Lepke, or stick with the mob.

The pressure was enormous, and Albert decided to double cross his friend. He told him that crooked lawyers working for the mob had made a deal, meaning that if Lepke turned himself in he would only have to serve a few years in prison. Lepke believed him – why wouldn't he? Albert was his friend.

Except, for Albert, he no longer was.

Lepke was sent down for 30 years, and Albert had one less ally in the mafia.[21]

Abe Reles

A historical murder came back into the spotlight when a witness came forward against Murder Inc.'s Abe Reles. Reles had been the one to overhear the conversation concerning the shooting of Morris

Diamond, and when he was arrested he decided to spill the beans on the mob to save his own skin. The information he supplied secured the conviction of seven of Murder Inc.'s hitmen. It also sent Lepke Buchalter to the electric chair.

Albert was furious and set a price on Reles' head. He knew that Reles' testimony could put him away, and he wanted him dead. Co-conspirators in a case couldn't testify against each other, but Abe Reles hadn't been part of the plot to murder Diamond when he overheard the conversation, so he was free to give evidence against Albert. With Anastasia in hiding, Reles gave more and more information to the police, leading the press to dub Albert 'The Mad Hatter'.

Knowing the mob's propensity for making witnesses disappear, Reles was hidden in a hotel and was under heavy 24-hour watch. But, on November 12th, 1941, Reles was found dead on the roof of the Half Moon Hotel, several storeys below his room. As far as the public was concerned, he had fallen to his death while trying to escape. Unofficially it was believed that he was pushed.

Once again, Anastasia escaped prosecution and certain death by electric chair and was free to return to the mob.

The case against him was dropped.[22]

The Army

In 1942, Albert Anastasia joined the army. His role was training men to be longshoremen, and a year later he was granted US citizenship for his service to the country. The following year he was honourably discharged due to his age.

Vincent Mangano

Albert had been running Murder Inc. until the mob decided, in light of the attention it had received as a result of Reles' information, to dissolve the group. He returned to the docks, as underboss to Vincent Mangano. It was common knowledge that it was an unhappy alliance, and, while Mangano was the boss in name, it was actually Anastasia who was in charge of criminal undertakings on the waterfront.

He began to make serious money from the gambling rackets which went on and bought a huge mansion in New Jersey. But it wasn't enough to satisfy the former head of Murder Inc., and he hatched a new plan.

When Luciano had laid down a new set of rules for the mob back in the early 1930s, one of those rules was that a mob boss would never be killed. The power-hungry Anastasia ignored that rule. Mangano was standing in the way of his supreme rule, and he wanted him gone.

In March 1951 the FBI was looking for Mangano in connection with mob activities, but he had disappeared. It was supposed that, in order to evade questioning, he had left town and was in hiding. Suspicions were raised when Vincent's brother, Philip, was found dead in a Brooklyn swamp sometime later. The Manganos were no more, and Anastasia took what he felt was his rightful position at the head of the Mangano family.

However, the slaughter of Philip Mangano and the supposed murder of Vincent (his body was never found) angered other mob members. Anastasia claimed that Mangano had taken out a contract on his head, and the killings had been simply a 'kill or be killed' scenario. Given the history between the two men, Albert's story was accepted.

But it was enough to sow the seeds of doubt all the same. There were those who believed that a man who could kill his own boss was not to be trusted.

Albert Anastasia had not finished breaking Luciano's code.

Arnold Schuster

Another of Luciano's rules was that civilians were off limits to the mob. But when Anastasia heard about a young man named Arnold Schuster who had led police to a bank robber on the run, he was furious.

In 1942, Schuster saw Willie Sutton, the fugitive bank robber, on the subway and knew the police were looking for him. He gave the police Sutton's whereabouts, which led to the arrest of the robber. Sutton had nothing to do with organized crime and was not affiliated with the mob in any way, but Albert hated those who gave information to the police. He sent a couple of his hitmen to find the 24-year-old Schuster and kill him.

The rest of the mob was left reeling, and angry. They had grudgingly given Albert the benefit of the doubt over the Mangano brothers, but now he had broken a second cardinal rule. Anastasia was out of control.

The murder was never solved, but it heralded the beginning of the end for Albert Anastasia.

Another mob leader, Vito Genovese, began drumming up opposition to Albert and managed to persuade Anastasia's underboss, Carlo Gambino, to change allegiance.

More Trouble

The following years brought more trouble for Anastasia. In 1953 his criminal activity saw him facing a deportation order which ended with a hung jury. A second trial date was set. But, as with many other cases involving Anastasia, the witnesses were picked off one by one. The second trial was heard in 1955, and Anastasia was sentenced to one year in prison with a plea bargain.[23]

Anastasia's Assassination

Vito Genovese capitalized on Anastasia's breaking of the rules. When he had killed his own boss, he had paved the way for others to do the same, and now Genovese wanted Albert dead. All hits were supposed to be given the go-ahead by The Commission, and Genovese took his concerns to them. They agreed to the hit.

Anastasia's days were numbered.

On October 25th, 1957, Albert Anastasia went to his barber at 10 o clock in the morning. The barber was situated within the Park

Sheraton Hotel. Anastasia sat in seat number four – the only seat in the barber's which afforded 360-degree views of his surroundings. But with a hot towel draped around his face, and his bodyguard taking a 'convenient' walk, Anastasia was temporarily vulnerable and unable to see the two masked gunmen approaching his chair. With two bullets in his body, he jumped from the chair. He saw the two men in the mirror, and with blood draining from his body, in his confusion he ran at their reflections. More shots were fired, and Albert Anastasia collapsed on the floor, dying.[24]

An Outcast

When Albert Anastasia was laid to rest on October 28th, 1957 at Brooklyn's Greenwood Cemetery, only 12 people paid their respects. The notable absence of the mafia was a sure sign of their rejection of the man as one of them.

Nobody was ever caught for his murder – the mafia was too clever and thorough to leave any evidence, and despite the murder taking place in broad daylight, no witnesses ever came forward.[25]

"Anastasia was an evil monster, he was a ferocious animal, he was a killing machine with no soul, he was a cold-blooded homicidal maniac, and he was a vicious, heartless, merciless, monstrous and deranged psychopathic killer. Anastasia had ice cold, vicious and devilish eyes, he had a look to put the fear of the devil in anybody."[26]

Albert Anastasia lived by the sword, and he died by the sword.

CLARENCE "THE PREACHER" HEATLEY

ISAAC WILLIAMS

Clarence "Preacher" Heatley struck fear into the hearts of New Yorkers for over a decade. He was the vicious, ruthless leader of the Preacher crew, a gang that specialized in drug trafficking, extortion, and intimidation. The gang allegedly called Heatley "Preacher" because of his dazzling way with words, and ability to manipulate people into following and fearing him. Heatley didn't only rule the streets through speeches, though. He threatened and intimidated his rivals and enemies. Dissenters would be beaten or murdered. Heatley became a local legend. Although nobody could describe him or knew his movements, everyone knew who he was and everyone was afraid of him. His name on the streets became The Black Hand of Death.

Sergeant James Maher of the NYPD said of Preacher's reputation, "You could walk up to anybody in the 32nd precinct, no matter how church-going they are, no matter if they're businessmen or local drug dealers, they all have a Preacher story, they all know who Preacher is. Ask any of them to describe Preacher to you, they're not going to be able to, because this guy was an infamous legend in Harlem."

Like with most legendary figures, not much is known about Heatley's early life or origins. He was born in the early 1950's in Harlem, New York. His life of crime started early. His formal education ended in the fourth grade, and he spent much of his youth in and out of juvenile detention centers.

By the time he was 30, Heatley had grown into a wildly intimidating presence. His charisma and knowledge of the streets, coupled with his 6'7" body and muscular build gave him everything he needed to take over Harlem. He established the Preacher crew in 1983. He took advantage of the crack epidemic that sprung up in New York in the 80's and began running drugs in the New York neighborhoods of Harlem and the Bronx.

Preacher ran his crew with military precision. He didn't allow them to take the drugs they were selling, nobody was allowed to steal from other members of the crew, no in-fighting was tolerated, and if someone crossed the crew they were to get revenge. Many people have described the Preacher crew as cult-like. Indeed, they had some characteristic hallmarks of a cult: a charismatic leader, a system of people below that leader who did not question his authority, and harsh punishments for dissenters or enemies of the group.

An anonymous former member of the Preacher crew had a harsher opinion of him. She didn't believe he was worthy of cult-leader status. She didn't even respect him as a gang leader. She said, "he's not even worthy to be called a gangster. Monster is a better fit."

Though he was definitely the leader, Preacher didn't run his crew alone. Where he was the head of the organization, and the mastermind behind many crimes, his right hand man John Cuff did most of the dirty work. Cuff was a former housing police officer, from 1982 to 1986. Some officers involved in gang activity start out clean and turn dirty, but Cuff joined the force to cover up his crimes, and gain more influence in the community. His badge was useful to the crew, as he was able to more easily extort money from rival dealers, intimidate people with his authority, and get Preacher out of jams with the police. Cuff worked closely with Preacher while he was an officer, and became his main lieutenant after he left the force.

As time went on, the crew expanded their empire. They went from just selling drugs, to creating a vast kidnapping and extortion racket. He allegedly took on contracts to kill people who had crossed dealers from other gangs. He would be paid between $100,000 and $300,000 for the hit, then would beat or kill the dealer who gave him the original contract, and take over their gang. He saw handing off personal vendettas to other gangs to take care of as a sign of weakness and cowardice. In his mind they didn't deserve to run a crew. He wanted what they had, so he took it.

Preacher also extorted large sums of money from other dealers. They paid him taxes of $10,000 just to be left alone. He would often go into local stores and steal all the money from the register. When the police showed up to take a statement, the owner of the store was always too scared to talk. Though they were visibly beaten or injured, they would tell the police they didn't have any information on who committed the crime. Creating a solid case against Preacher that would lead to an arrest was becoming increasingly difficult, as he expanded his sphere of influence, and intimidated entire neighborhoods.

Preacher may even have been involved in a high profile kidnapping. Dave Collins, a former gang member, recalled a legendary tale in his book *Preacher of the Streets*, an autobiography about his time in the Preacher crew. Famous R&B artist Bobby Brown allegedly owed $25,000 to a New Jersey drug dealer. This dealer knew of Preacher, and his nefarious tactics to extort money from his enemies and competitors. He approached Preacher and told him of the debt that Brown was refusing to pay him. Preacher then bought the debt from the man for the opportunity to deal with Brown himself.

Brown was approached by Preacher crew members at a Manhattan nightclub and given high quality cocaine for free. He was then lured to a Bronx apartment the crew was using for gang related activities. Brown was accosted, stripped, hogtied, and threatened with death.

Collins remembers, "The Preacher left the room and his men then terrorised Bobby for two hours. They kicked him. They told him they would kill Whitney. One of them put a gun to his head. Bobby was weeping when the Preacher came back in the room, begging the Preacher to let him call Whitney."

Brown was allowed to call his then-wife Whitney Houston. He told her of the threat to his life; then Preacher took the phone and made a deal with Houston. Instead of the $25,000 Brown owed, Preacher asked for $400,000. The next day, Houston came to Preacher in disguise and handed over the exorbitant amount of money in exchange for her husband's life. Neither Brown nor Houston addressed this rumour publicly when Collins' book came out, leading many to believe it is, in fact, true. It certainly fits with Preacher's tactics. Heatley was no stranger to extortion, kidnapping, or death threats. The fact that Brown even made it out alive made him one of the lucky ones.

The road to capturing Heatley began with the tragic story of 12-year-old Donnell Porter. On December 5th, 1989, Donnell was kidnapped from the street as he walked the short four blocks from his home to his school, in Harlem. When Donnell didn't come home from school that day his family began to worry. They then received a series of phone calls, one demanding a $500,000 ransom for Donnell's safe return, on the condition the family not involve the police.

Donnell's mother, Velma, told the person on the other end of the line that the family could not afford the ransom. The next day the family received another call from the kidnapper who both lowered the ransom to $350,000, and told the family to go to the McDonald's at 125th and Broadway. In the bathroom they would find evidence that the kidnappers really had Donnell, and that their ransom demands were serious. A family friend went to the spot the kidnapper specified. He found a coffee can that contained a cassette tape, two of Donnell's rings, and a bloody piece of the boy's index finger.

Donnell's voice was on the tape. He was crying for help and urging his family to find the ransom money, or his kidnappers would further mutilate him. The kidnappers called again, and the family insisted they could only pay $200,000. The kidnapper told the Porter family they would call back in ten minutes, but the panicked family never received another call. They had no other option but to involve the authorities. That night, against the instructions of the kidnappers, the Porter's called the police.

The family insisted to the police they didn't know who could be involved in the kidnapping. The police, however, were aware that Donnell's brother, Richard Porter, was the head of a central Harlem drug gang. Police began questioning Rich Porter, and members of his gang about Donnell's kidnapping. Most were tight-lipped, but some began to float the name Preacher as a possible suspect. One said,

"Maybe it was one of the big drug dealers Richard owed money to, I don't know; maybe it was Alpo, or John-John, or Lou from 142nd Street...maybe it was Preacher."

On December 10th, five days after Donnell's disappearance, the Porter family received a letter from a neighborhood child, who had gotten it from an unknown woman on the street. The letter simply said, "We still want the money the child is in pain and he needs medical attention."

On January 3rd, 1990, Rich Porter was murdered. His body was found in a park in the Bronx. He had $2,239 in his pocket, all his jewelry was still in place, and his car was parked nearby. With so many expensive things to steal still on the body, the police knew the murder had to have been committed for personal reasons, rather than for some sort of financial gain. Porter's business partner Albert "Alpo" Martinez was later discovered to have killed him. Though he confessed to that murder, he maintained he knew nothing about Donnell's kidnapping. On January 28th, 1990, Donnell's body was found, dismembered, frozen from the cold, and scattered near the same park where his brother's body was dumped. He had been killed by blunt force trauma to the head.

Police began putting more pressure on Preacher crew members. Donnell and Rich's own uncle, Johnnie "Apple" Porter, was a dealer with the Preacher crew. According to an interview with Preacher's own son, Shaka, Apple had approached Preacher saying he could extort a large sum of money from Rich Porter if he kidnapped Donnell. Preacher gave the go-ahead for the plan. Apple and Maalik, an ex-military man and higher-up in the crew, carried out the kidnapping and began making ransom calls to the family.

When Rich died, Preacher knew the family would have no way of raising the ransom money. He also knew he couldn't let Donnell live, or he would be identified and arrested. Preacher ordered the murder of Donnell Porter, which was carried out by Maalik. It became obvious that nothing was off limits to Preacher; not even children, or family members. While in custody, Johnnie Porter confessed to five other murders he had been involved in. He went to prison for life.

Partly in response to Preacher's violent, unruly conduct, and to contend with the booming drug trade in general, the FBI and the NYPD had created the C-11 task force. It was focused on bringing down criminal conspiracy gangs. These gangs had become too big, too involved, and too smart to be dealt with on a state level. Authorities needed access to both federal resources, and federal courts to make cases against big time drug runners

In April of 1994 an informant from the Preacher crew, Larry "Love" Jones, came forward to speak to C-11. Two of his closest colleagues had already been murdered and he was afraid he was next. He told the officers what he knew about Preacher's organization, and the crimes he had committed. Some of Jones' information even lead to years-old cold cases being solved.

Jones told C-11 of Preacher's killing basement at an apartment building, located at 2075 Grand Concourse. Preacher ran the basement like an ancient Roman court. He held trial for those who had wronged him or the crew. Those in attendance voted with a thumbs up or a thumbs down. If the majority of the people voting showed a thumbs down, the person on trial would be killed.

Then the crew's "janitors" would clean up the mess from the murder, and be responsible for disposing of the body. They often dismembered the bodies of the victims so they would be easier to dispose of, and harder to identify. They then wiped down the walls and floors with boric acid to ensure there were no traces of blood left behind. Being a janitor for Preacher was an important and coveted position. Like many gang initiations, men had to actually murder someone themselves in order to become a janitor for the crew, and have the twisted honor of ensuring no evidence of a murder was left behind.

This brutal basement court system wasn't only used on enemies of the crew. Many internal murders happened there as well. Maalik, the man in charge of the janitors, and the man ultimately responsible for Donnell Porter's death, was murdered in the basement before he could be brought to justice for ending the child's life. Preacher believed Maalik was out of control. He was becoming a liability to the crew; lying, carrying out deals and killings not sanctioned by Preacher. He was clearly vying to knock Cuff out of his coveted spot as Preacher's main lieutenant, and perhaps even wanted to dethrone Preacher himself.

Maalik had begun attempting to undermine Cuff to Preacher, and saying they should kill Cuff before he gets out of hand. Preacher, however, had another plan. He was growing weary of Maalik using his name to commit crimes he hadn't signed off on. The man had to be taken out. On March 21st, 1994, he was lured to the killing basement of 2075 Grand Concourse under the pretence of following through with his plan to kill Cuff. Once in the basement, Maalik was asked to turn up the radio. As he bent down to reach the knob, he was shot in the head and died instantly.

The janitors went to work cleaning up the remains of their boss. They dismembered his body with a circular saw, and burned the parts of him that showed gang-related tattoos, so that, if his remains were found, he would not be tied back to Preacher. Shaka, Preacher's son, later said in an interview that members of the crew were so depraved, bloodthirsty, and disconnected from any semblance of decency, that they went to the roof of the building with Maalik's head wrapped up in a sheet, and used it as a soccer ball.

Larry Jones continued to work with C-11 as an informant. After leaving a meeting at a Manhattan courthouse Jones spotted Preacher and Cuff in a van. He knew they would have no reason to be there, and realized they knew he had been informing on the crew. Jones knew his life was in danger. He called his handlers in C-11 then took off in his car going the wrong way down the avenue. The van followed him.

When the C-11 officers and agents showed up to the scene they arrested Heatley, Cuff, and two other crew members for reckless endangerment. They searched the van the crew was using and found rope, knives, masks, and personal information on Jones. C-11 was certain the crew members were at the courthouse to follow and kill Jones that day. However, they could not definitively prove that was their plan, and had to let them out of their custody soon after their arrest.

From that point on Preacher started to close ranks. He now knew the FBI was after him because agents had been present at his arrest. C-11's attempts to get an undercover agent into the crew failed. They couldn't get a man anywhere close to Preacher.

In the weeks that followed Preacher became increasingly paranoid. He was always talking about how he knew the FBI was watching him, and it was a matter of time before they came for him. He began to distrust John Cuff, the man who had loyally carried out all his orders for years.

His paranoia over Cuff did not turn out to be entirely unfounded. The informant Larry Jones told C-11 about the death of Sheila Berry, a former drug runner for the crew. Cuff allegedly didn't want to pay the supplier Sheila dealt with, and decided to tell Preacher that Sheila was stealing their drugs. She was a known drug addict and was working with the crew for a steady supply, but she was not, in fact stealing. Regardless, in January of 1995 she was lured to the killing basement and murdered.

Jones told the authorities about two abandoned apartment buildings at 104 and 108 Bradhurst Avenue that the crew used as a dumping ground for victims' bodies. The apartments were thoroughly searched, to the point that parts of the buildings were cut away to ensure every inch could be seen. There they found Sheila's body. Jones' information also lead to authorities finding Maalik's body, dismembered and burned, just like Jones said.

Confirming Jones' stories with the physical evidence was a gruesome but necessary step in arresting Preacher and his crew. The FBI also checked out the infamous basement of 2075 Grand Concourse that their informant had told them about. Though the crew's janitors were fairly thorough with their clean-ups, it is almost impossible to remove all traces of such brutal crimes from a room. Using luminol, a chemical that reacts to traces of hemoglobin in the leftover blood of a crime scene, agents were able to confirm that bloody murders had taken place there, thereby confirming Jones' tales of Preacher's killing basement.

Thanks in large park to the informant's cooperation, C-11 had amassed a 47 count indictment against Preacher that included 11 murders, as well as drug trafficking and conspiracy charges.

The Racketeer Influenced and Corrupt Organizations Act, or RICO for short, was enacted in America in 1970 in an attempt to deal with the mounting mob threats to major cities in the U.S. Originally devised to take down Mafia families, RICO eventually expanded to include other organized groups that may commit a series of related crimes. Drug gangs, pro-life activists, and even the international football federation, FIFA, have all been prosecuted under RICO laws.

If a person has committed "at least two acts of racketeering activity" from a list of 35 different offences in the last ten years, they can be prosecuted under RICO laws, provided that the offenses are all related to a criminal enterprise. Such offenses include Preacher's wheelhouses of extortion, kidnapping, murder, and dealing in controlled substances.

In the case of drug gangs like the Preacher crew, RICO ensures the head of the organization can be brought up on charges, even though that person may not have been directly involved in any of the crimes. It is possible that Heatley didn't kidnap or murder anyone himself, but he was the mastermind behind the crimes, and he ordered them done, so he was guilty.

Once arrested, Heatley immediately confessed to his crimes. On February 6th, 1999, Clarence Heatley pleaded guilty to being involved in 13 murders. He also informed on all of his subordinates. He gave up the names of his entire crew, even including his own son and daughter. Thanks to Heatley's information, fifteen people were sought in connection to the crew's crimes, though four were never found.

Usually those who inform on other people, and give the government information that leads to solving open cases get a 5K1 letter that reduces their sentence. Because of the brutal nature of his crimes, though, Preacher wasn't offered this kindness. Instead, the Department of Justice advised that the death penalty should be sought for both Heatley and Cuff. If the cases went to trial they would have been the first instances of federal death penalty cases in New York state in over 40 years, and the first instance of a former police officer facing execution in over 70 years.

After hours of stories from Preacher where he detailed the ins and outs of his crimes as best he could, his lawyers wondered if it was even ethical to seek a plea deal for him. He had ordered so many horrific things he could barely remember who he wanted killed, why he wanted them out of the way, who carried out the hit, or where the bodies were. Heatley, however, did get a plea deal. He would simply plead guilty to all the charges brought against him. That way there would be no need for a jury trial, and no chance of being sentenced to death.

Those involved in the case believed he only admitted to everything in order to avoid a trial that would almost certainly end in him being sentenced to death. Joel S. Cohen, one of Heatley's lawyers said, "There didn't seem to be any upside to going to trial if we could be certain that he would avoid execution by pleading guilty." Cohen continued to explain that Heatley wanted to spare his family "from having to experience his execution, and he also wanted to try to be a positive presence in the lives of his children."

This defense, though, seemed to be in opposition to the fact that he gave his children's names to police during his lengthy confession. Many see his cooperation with authorities as a cowardly betrayal of his crew; giving over everyone who had been so loyal to him just to save his own life. He apparently showed no remorse for any of the crimes he committed saying simply, "Yes, Your Honor, I did direct them to be killed" when he was asked about the victims of the killing basement.

In an extremely uncharacteristic moment during his sentencing, Heatley appeared bashful and embarrassed while his charges were being read. When the judge noticed this behavior Heatley gestured to the benches of the court, where his mother sat. It appeared the violent, remorseless gang leader who had terrorized the streets of Harlem for years didn't want his mother to know what he had been up to. Clarence Heatley received life in prison, plus 225 years.

On March 23rd 1999, Cuff also pleaded guilty to his involvement in 10 murders. He, too, showed no remorse for his involvement in his crimes, even interrupting an attorney to say that he had strangled a certain victim to death, when she had mistakenly said he shot the victim. Like Preacher, Cuff avoided a trial and took a plea that would send him to jail for life, instead of facing the death penalty.

Heatley's brother, William Mack, disagreed with the terms of the RICO charges. He said, "It's not fair. A lot of the charges belong to other people." That is, though, the point of RICO laws. Though he may not have laid his hands on anyone himself, Clarence Heatley was still brought to justice, and given the sentence he deserved, for years of ordering the beatings, kidnappings, extortions, and murders of the innocent citizens of his own neighborhood.

Heatley's own son also ended up in jail, thanks to his father. With a father like Preacher Shaka had no chance of avoiding a life of crime. He was born into it. He said he was part of a group within the crew that would commit murders for his father. While Preacher had confessed to being involved with 13 murders, his son later said the crew was more likely responsible for between 50 and 70 killings during Preacher's reign.

U.S. Attorney Mary Jo White summed up the crew pretty well, "They were very good at what they did and they always made an effort to make sure there were no witnesses...They were careful. They were smart and they intimidated all those around them, drug dealers and citizens alike." Regardless of the eventual outcome, it is clear that the Preacher crew made a huge, unforgettable mark on Harlem, New York.

TOUGH TONY

JESSI DILMAN

Mafia enforcer Anthony "Tough Tony" Spilotro was the main muscle protecting the Chicago mafia's illegal casino profits in Las Vegas in the 1970s and 1980s, until his death in 1986. Spilotro's time in Las Vegas, and the circumstances surrounding his murder, inspired the memorable character Nicky Santoro, played by Joe Pesci in Martin Scorsese's 1995 film *Casino*.

"Ya know, he just – he was just a man, and got caught up in some things that maybe he shouldn't have," said Spilotro's son Vincent, "but he lived it the way he lived it."

At only five feet six inches tall and weighing no more than 160 pounds, Spilotro didn't have the look of an intimidating gangster. In fact, he seemed more like a businessman than a mob boss, earning nicknames like "Tony the Ant" and "The Little Guy." But the detached confidence that lurked menacingly behind his blue eyes betrayed the darkness hidden just below the surface.

While he managed to quickly claw his way to the top of the Chicago mafia ranks in spite of his somewhat meek physical appearance, Spilotro's reign came to an end just as fast. After just a decade and a half as the "overlord of Sin City," he wound up falling victim to his own paranoia, ambition, and violent disposition.

Breaking the law

In Chicago on May 19, 1938, Anthony Spilotro (pronounced Spil-ah-tro) was the fourth of six children born to Italian parents. Pasquale had come to America in 1914 after leaving a town in the Italian province of Bari called Triggiano, and married a young woman named Antoinette. Together, the couple ran Patsy's restaurant – famous for delicious homemade meatballs that brought in customers from all across the city.

The restaurant was regularly frequented by mobsters, including Sam Giancana, Jackie Cerone, Gussie Alex, and Frank "The Enforcer" Nitti. They would also use the restaurant's parking lot as a mob meeting place.

Perhaps this exposure to criminal activity was what led to Spilotro's involvement in petty crime from a young age. While one of his brothers, Pasquale, eventually became one of the Chicago area's most well-respected oral surgeons, the other Spilotro brothers – John, Vincent, Victor, Michael, and Anthony, were less driven to succeed. By the time Spilotro dropped out of Steinmetz High School in Chicago during his sophomore year, he was already earning a reputation as a law-breaker.

By 1955, Spilotro had already experienced his first arrest. On January 11, an attempt to steal a watch from a store in River Forest landed him a larceny charge. The young Spilotro was fined just $10, and placed on probation.

Once the 1960s rolled around, Spilotro found himself in more hot water with the law. He pled guilty to the charge of attempted bribery, which had apparently been carried out with a player on the New York University basketball team, in advance of a game against West Virginia University. Spilotro is also suspected to have attempted to bribe a football player from the University of Oregon, as well.

Spilotro's arrests at that time were primarily for minor offenses, but he was starting to build relationships with underworld figures who were beginning to climb the ranks of the Chicago mob. He was first linked with Frank "Lefty" Rosenthal, but developed connections to Joseph Aiuppa, Joseph Lombardo, William Daddano Sr., and Jimmy "The Turk" Torrello. He also found mentorship from "Mad" Sam DeStefano, followed by Felix "Milwaukee Phil" Alderisio and Charles Nicoletti.

By 1963, Spilotro was a made member of the Chicago mafia. His first assignment was with a large bookmaking operation, but he also worked for a time as a bail bondsman for a noted mafia associate, Irwin "Red" Weiner.

Spilotro's first major run-in with the law was in November, 1963, when a former associate of Sam DeStefano's provided the FBI with evidence implicating Spilotro and DeStefano in the murder of a real estate agent and loan collector, Leo Foreman. Both Spilotro and DeStefano were acquitted, however.

Voyage to Vegas

By 1971, Spilotro had earned himself enough of a reputation as mafia muscle that he landed a position in Las Vegas, replacing Marshall Caifano as the Chicago mob's local representation. According to Assistant State's Attorney Paul Nealis, Spilotro had quickly become "the liason between Chicago organized crime and organized crime in Las Vegas.

Reunited with his childhood friend Frank "Lefty" Rosenthal, Spilotro soon started looking for ways to make extra cash on the side.

"Those people were separately their own entrepreneurs," said former gaming control board member Jeff Silver. "In the case of Tony Spilotro, the Hole in the Wall gang, the robberies, the burglaries, and the loan sharking that came with it, they had free reign to do whatever they wanted – as long as it didn't create too much notoriety."

Rosenthal ran a number of casinos backed by the mafia, including the Stardust. Together, the pair began embezzling money from the casinos' profits ("the skim"), and sent the money to the homes of mafia families in the midwest, particularly families in Chicago.

"(Spilotro) did a lot of things he was not supposed to do that were really bad for business and for the Outfit," said John Binder, who wrote about the mafia family in his book "The Chicago Outfit."

Using the alias Tony Stuart, Spilotro began running the gift shop at the "family" oriented Circus-Circus Hotel on the Las Vegas strip. His $70,000 investment in the property paid off quickly – by 1974, the hotel was sold, and Spilotro received $700,000 back.

In 1976, Spilotro invested his profit by opening his own business. The Gold Rush Ltd., which he opened with his brother Michael and top lieutenant Herbert "Fat Herbie" Blitzstein, was just one block off the strip. The combination jewelry store and "electronics factory" gave

Blitzstein and the Spilotros the opportunity to earn valuable experience in the fencing of stolen goods.

Years later, Cullotta testified that Spilotro had in fact been receiving a cut from all of the burglaries and robberies taking place in Las Vegas at the time. An investigation that took place after Spilotro was murdered revealed that he'd purchased "extensive" properties throughout the city.

"He told me in 1978 when I first arrived in Las Vegas that no one was to know that he was getting a cut, because he didn't want any problems with the people back in Chicago," Cullotta told the court.

Spilotro was known for his habit of terrorizing his underlings. While the tactic was intended as an attempt to secure their loyalty to the Chicago Outfit, it would often have the opposite effect – often leading the associates to seek protection from the authorities and federal agents. He would also bad mouth the higher-up Chicago mobsters he worked for, which eventually led to his downfall.

Drilling holes

Spilotro and Michael also teamed up with Blitzstein to start a burglary ring that would provide the goods to be sold at The Gold Rush. Eight other associates joined the gang, which quickly earned a reputation as the "Hole in the Wall Gang" because of their distinctive ability to gain entry to the buildings they burglarized by drilling through the exterior walls or ceilings.

The group was comprised of the two Spilotro brothers, "Fat Herbie," Samuel Cusumano, Joseph Cusumano, Ernesto "Ernie" Davino, Lawrence "Crazy Larry" Neumann, Wayne Matecki, Salvatore "Sonny" Romano, Leonardo "Leo" Guardino, Frank Cullotta, and Joseph Blasko, a former Las Vegas detective who served as a lookout for the gang.

A botched attempted robbery at a Las Vegas jewelry store marked the beginning of the end for the gang. Sal Romano had been assigned to do counter-surveillance during the burglary at a store called Bertha's Household Products. The heist was planned for July 4.

When the group showed up at Bertha's to commit the crime, though, police and federal agents were already there waiting. Romano had turned informant months before the planned heist.

Blasko, Guardino, Cullotta, Matecki, Davino, and Neumann all faced multiple charges, including burglary, conspiracy to commit burglary, possession of burglary tools, and grand larceny. Following the arrests, the gang members were held at the Las Vegas police department's downtown holding cell.

Bitter betrayal

As Spilotro was working his way up with the Chicago mob, his childhood friend Frank Cullotta was right behind him – doing most of Spilotro's dirty work, including the murders of James Miraglia and Billy McCarthy in 1962.

The slayings were known as the "M&M Murders," and had been ordered by Spilotro following an attack in a neighbourhood in suburban Chicago that was home to several members of the mafia outfit. The area was considered off-limits for murders and other criminal activity, since it may attract the unwanted attention of the authorities to the seemingly quiet neighbourhood. However, Miraglia and McCarthy robbed and killed three businessmen there – and Spilotro wanted revenge.

By the 1980s, Cullotta had been implicated in a number of crimes, and was a primary suspect in a 1979 murder in Las Vegas where mob associate Sherwin "Jerry" Lisner was killed. He was finally arrested in November of 1981 on an indictment for possession of stolen property – furniture stolen in a previous burglary of a woman's house was discovered in Cullotta's home.

Cullotta was incarcerated, and according to mob protocol, Spilotro was responsible for supporting Cullotta's family during his associate's time in prison. However, authorities learned that Spilotro had instead ordered a hit on both Cullotta and another burglar, Wayne Matecki.

Hole in the Wall gang member Lawrence Neumann planned to post bail for Cullotta, then murder the two burglars once Cullotta was out. But the police were already wise to Spilotro's scheme, and revoked Cullotta's bail to keep him safe. In return, Cullotta spilled the details of the "M&M Murders."

Eventually, Cullotta was sentenced to eight years for the charges relating to the stolen property – and based on his testimony, Spilotro was indicted less than a year later. In September of 1983, he was brought in by the Las Vegas police on the charges of murder and racketeering.

Spilotro's trial for the slayings of Miraglia and McCarthy took him back to Chicago, before Cook County Circuit Judge Thomas J. Maloney. Neumann received a sentence of life in prison for his role in the failed executions of Cullotta and Matecki, but Spilotro managed to get himself acquitted of the charges. According to Maloney, Cullotta's statements weren't sufficient evidence and proof beyond a reasonable doubt – but during Operation Greylord in 1992, the judge was convicted of having accepted bribes in a number of unrelated cases.

A murderous history

Throughout his life, Spilotro was implicated in a number of murders – in fact, the murder rate in Las Vegas jumped by 70 per cent after Spilotro moved to the area. However, his first hits took place back in Chicago, when Bill McCarthy and James Miraglia made the fatal mistake of robbing and killing businessmen in a mafia neighbourhood.

According to reports, the bodies were found in the trunk of a car on May 15, 1962, on the southwest side of Chicago. They'd been badly beaten, and both had slit throats. It is suspected that McCarthy had been caught first, and in an attempt to persuade him to give up Miraglia's whereabouts, his head had been placed in a vise that was tightened until his eye popped out.

Spilotro is also suspected to have been involved with a number of other murders, such as the attempted car bombing committed against Rosenthal on October 4, 1982 and the slaying of his former mentor DeStefano on April 15, 1973. Other possible victims include Tamara Rand, a Las Vegas real estate heiress; Allen Dorfman with the Teamsters Union; Sam Giancana, a onetime mob boss in the Chicago mafia; and Danny Siefert, the manager of a fibreglass company whose wife and four-year-old son watched as he was shot in cold blood in September of 1974.

Once he had secured sufficient influence in Las Vegas, Spilotro is believed to have killed Frank "the Bomp" Bompensiero. As the consigliere of California's "Mickey Mouse Mafia," the Cosa Nostra family outfit, Bompensiero was allegedly feeding information to the FBI – and the midwest mob bosses thought he was an embarrassment to the entire mafia.

Additional rumors circulated regarding Spilotro's involvement in the killing of William "Action" Jackson, a loan shark enforcer who had been employed by DeStefano throughout the 1950s and 1960s. By 1961, though, the Chicago mafia had started to suspect that Jackson was cooperating with the FBI – and allegedly, Spilotro took care of the situation.

Jackson's body was found hanging in a local meat packing plant by a meat hook which had been inserted in his rectum. His knees had been smashed, likely with a hammer, and according to reports, Spilotro had used an electric cattle prod on Jackson's genitals before leaving him on the edge of death. The medical examiner determined Jackson had suffered for three days before he finally succumbed to the extensive damage Spilotro had inflicted.

Blacklisted and targeted

While Rosenthal's job in Las Vegas was to manage the casinos, Spilotro was in charge of controlling the casino employees and personnel that had become involved in the skimming scheme – all the while maintaining his position as mob enforcer and operating The Gold Rush with his partners.

"He was essentially operating on his own," said former FBI supervisor John Mallul. "Keeping the proceeds to himself and not looking for authority to do anything."

Spilotro's reign over Las Vegas wouldn't last long. In December of 1979, the Nevada Gaming Commission (chaired at the time by Senate Majority Leader Harry Reid) blacklisted Spilotro.

The ruling came as a direct consequence of testimony provided by Aaladena "Jimmy The Weasel" Fratianno, after he was arrested in 1977. For Spilotro, the decision was devastating – he was legally prevented from being physically present in any casino in the entire state of Nevada. Spilotro also soured his relationship with Rosenthal when he started up an affair with his associate's wife, Geraldine McGee.

By October 1932, federal investigators had collected enough evidence to indict Spilotro and more than a dozen other midwest crime family racketeers for their involvement with the multi-million-dollar casino skimming operation. As a result of the indictments, the money that had been flowing from Las Vegas into the mob outfit essentially halted – and the massive loss was primarily attributed to Spilotro's mistakes.

"The United States of America versus Anthony Spilotro," he is quoted as stating. "Now, what kind of odds are those?"

Still, Spilotro managed to evade prison once again. In April 1986, the judge declared a mistrial – and as prosecutors began preparing for a second attempt at a conviction, a new mob boss was taking over the Chicago outfit.

With Joe Ferriola now in charge of the Chicago crime family, it was decided that Spilotro would need to be taken out. According to an article that ran in the Chicago Tribune on June 25, 1986, investigators believed Spilotro had been "marked for death" as many as three months before he was finally killed.

Loans were being called in from mob sharks in Las Vegas, Los Angeles, and San Diego during the three months leading up to Spilotro's death – the Chicago outfit collected an estimated $1.5 million, supposedly to pay for legal fees. However, according to some sources, the mob was "clearing the books" because the bosses knew Spilotro wouldn't be around much longer.

"Tony's caused the Outfit a lot of problems, and he'd stopped generating money. Michael is cocky and has caused problems, too," Frank Cullotta remembers saying when he heard the brothers were missing. "They aren't needed anymore. If you whack one, you gotta whack them both. I guarantee you, they're both dead."

Sam "Wings" Carlisi is suspected to have contacted Spilotro and his brother Michael, to invite them to a hunting lodge owned by Joey "The Doves" Aiuppa – Spilotro's former mafia boss, who was in prison at the time. Testimony provided by Spilotro's associates revealed that Aiuppa was furious about Spilotro's blatant affair with McGee.

"I don't care how you do it," he allegedly ordered. "Get him. I want him out."

Carlisi had told the Spilotro brothers that they were going to be recognized by the family for their efforts – Spilotro would be receiving a promotion, while Michael would finally become a "made man" and earn an official spot with the Chicago outfit. However, when the brothers arrived for the supposed meeting, they were savagely beaten and buried in an Enos, Indiana cornfield. After the bodies were found June 23 by an area farmer, they were identified by Pasquale Spilotro Jr. – through dental records.

"It's very likely that the persons responsible for this left the scene of the crime with the anticipation that the bodies would never be found," said Ed Hegarty, the FBI's special agent in charge in Chicago – adding that the killers' effort to conceal the grave was a "botched attempt," as the shoots of corn in the new field were just four inches high at the time of the burial.

Still, this isn't the first time murderers have tried to dispose of corpses in Newton County. Since 1980, authorities have uncovered eight different bodies in this small section of northwestern Indiana.

"It just seems like we're the dumping place for bodies from up north," said Jackie Allis with the county welfare office. "It seems like it's happening more... we're not very heavily populated, so it's easy to get rid of a body."

The autopsy revealed that there was sand left in the lungs of the two brothers, indicating that they may have been buried alive. The investigation into the murders led the FBI to believe that the brothers were beaten and strangled at the hunting lodge, which was located in DuPage County, Illinois – and then brought to Indiana, where they were buried. The coroner's estimation is that the brothers were killed June 14, the same day they left Oak Park.

Dr. John Pless, a forensic pathologist who took part in the autopsies, told the court that the multiple blunt trauma injuries both brothers had suffered to the head, neck, and chest were probably not caused by bats.

"It doesn't appear that an instrument was used because of the lack of fractures," said Newton County Coroner David Dennis, adding that the brothers had probably been beaten "with a fist or gloved hand," and repeatedly kicked.

Pless noted that the Spilotro brothers' airways were likely so full of blood that they couldn't breathe, which likely contributed to the cause of death – officially determined to be the extensive head and neck trauma. The bruises found on the backs of the Spilotro brothers' hands suggested that they had been trying to shield themselves from the multiple blows, Pless added.

According to Michael Spilotro's daughter Michelle, her father said he loved her "at least ten times" before he left the house with his brother on June 14. The Spilotro brothers also took off all of their valuables and personal identification prior to driving off in Michael's Lincoln Continental – possibly because they suspected they were being set up.

"He said if he wasn't back by nine o'clock, it was no good," Michael's wife, Ann, stated during the trial.

A burning car was discovered on June 16 along County Road 100 North – near the cornfield where the Spilotro brothers were buried. According to investigators, the car had been stolen from the south side of Chicago on June 14, the day the murders are believed to have taken place.

To keep investigators from finding incriminating evidence, including microscopic details like hairs or fibers, Hegarty said mafia outfits will frequently burn vehicles that have been used in murders. He believed the car may have been used to transport the bodies of the Spilotro brothers to the cornfield for disposal.

Search for justice

No one was arrested for the murders of the Spilotro brothers until April 25, 2005, when an investigation called Operation Family Secrets brought charges against 14 members of the Chicago outfit. They were indicted for a total of 18 different murders, including the two Spilotro brothers', in an effort by the government to deal with unsolved gang killings and take down the organized crime outfits in Chicago.

Albert Tocco was a key suspect, sentenced to twenty years in prison based on the testimony provided by his wife, Betty. On the day the Spilotros were murdered, she claimed, she received a call to pick her husband up just one mile away from where the bodies were eventually discovered. He'd been wearing dirty blue work clothes, she said, and had been with Nicholas "Nicky" Guzzino, Dominick "Tootsie" Palermo, and Albert "Chickie" Rovero.

Alleged assassin Frank "The German" Schweihs was also a suspect – not just in the murders of the Spilotro brothers, but in at least 70 other killings. Schweihs was a convicted burglar and an extortionist who already had two felony murder charges pending against him when he was arrested in December of 2005.

The conspiracy was blown open on May 18, 2007 – star witness Nicholas Calabrese pled guilty to involvement in 14 of the 18 mafia murders, including the killings of the two Spilotro brothers. Calabrese's testimony was delivered with extensive security protection, as he implicated his brother, Frank Calabrese Sr., and a number of other important mafia figures including Joey "the Clown" Lombardo, Paul "the Indian" Schiro, James Marcello, and Anthony "Twan" Doyle, a former Chicago police officer.

After the FBI used DNA evidence to link Calabrese to the Spilotro case, he is suspected to have agreed to provide testimony against the others. According to Calabrese's account of the Spilotro murders, the brothers were killed by Calabrese and several other members of the Chicago outfit – James LaPietra, John DiFronzo, James Marcello, John Fecarotta, Sam Carlisi, Louis Marino, Joseph Ferriola, Louie "The Mooch" Eboli, and Ernest "Rocky" Infelice.

"The plan was simply to tackle them, hold them down, and strangle them," said Mullul, but Binder added that many of the "top guys" were present to get "their whacks in" before the brothers were killed.

At the trial in 2007, Frank Calabrese Jr. described the event to the jury in more graphic detail – despite not having been present for the murder. The story, according to Frank, was relayed to him by his uncle, Nicholas Calabrese.

"He came into the basement and there were a whole bunch of guys who grabbed him and strangled him and beat him to death," he said. "Tony put up a fight. He kept saying, 'You guys are going to get in trouble, you guys are going to get in trouble.'"

Michael was the first one down the stairs, though, Nicholas Calabrese recalled. He told the jury that before he grabbed Michael's legs and held him down while "Louie the Mooch" put a rope around his neck, he'd said, "How are you doing, Mike?"

Despite their implication in the Spilotro murders, Ferriola, Marino, and Infelice attended a wake on June 26, the day before the brothers were buried in the family plot at Queen of Heaven Cemetery in Hillside.

"The convictions in the 'family secrets' case pretty much gutted what was left of the Chicago hierarchy," stated reporter George Knapp in an article published on Las Vegas Now. "In the years that followed, other mobsters tried to fill those shoes (left by the Spilotro brothers), but no one else came close."

However, the Spilotro legacy lives on through Martin Scorsese's *Casino*, a 1995 film that is loosely based on Spilotro's time working in Las Vegas with Rosenthal. Nicky Santoro, played by Joe Pesci, is a key antagonist throughout the movie – and during the climax of the film, Santoro and his brother Dominick are brutally beaten with baseball bats before being buried alive in a cornfield.

Spilotro also served as the inspiration for the character Ray Luca, a mobster in the television series *Crime Story*, which aired on NBC in the 1980s.

To this day, Las Vegas officials insist that the city is free from the traditional organized crime that was rampant during Spilotro's time skimming money from casinos on the strip.

"For the last fifteen years," said mayoral candidate and attorney Oscar Goodman, who had previously represented local mobsters – including Spilotro, "there hasn't been a mob presence here."

THE MURDER OF THERESA FERRARA

96

NATALIE FOGEL

Theresa Ferrara and the Lucchese Crime Family

New York in the 1970's was certainly one of the most crime driven cities in the world. The Lucchese family was one of "The Five" families that dominated the organized crime scene in this era. In fact, this family still holds great power today. Becoming involved with this family was never a matter of "if" you would run into problems, but rather "when". Through countless, calculated murders, crimes, and street wars, this family soon came to be feared by everyone that wasn't "made" or an "associate." Ultimately, the story of Theresa Ferrara is officially unsolved. What is fact and proven true is that Ferrara was involved and a major pawn in much of the Lucchese crime activity in the 70's. Her demise is one of great tragedy and a picture of what lengths the Lucchese family would go to in order to protect its goals.

Theresa Ferrara was not the typical Italian-American female. She was born in Long Island, New York in 1951. She was a gorgeous young woman who could hold her own in nearly any situation. To say that Mafia traditions were in her blood is a true and most literal statement. She was a relative of New Orleans crime boss Carlos Marcello. She did, however, have modest early goals for her life.

Ferrara moved to Queens, New York in her late teen years. She had long dreamed of being an actress and a model as a teenager. She had much support from her family in this endeavor. After all, her family new the possibilities of what may happen if she went down a path that others in her family had. Theresa would soon happen in to the Mafia circle by circumstance, rather than by her own initial intuition. An introduction at a bar in Queens, New York would ultimately start her path to a horrific fate.

The Lucchese family was one of "The Five" families that ran New York at this time. This organized crime ring was and still is a nationwide phenomenon known collectively by the group title as The Mafia. Among the five families, each had a share of New York that would control nearly every aspect of its area. Businesses were made to pay "dues" to the family whose area they were located in. This was not an optional due as the result for not paying said dues would not be a pleasant punishment. Drug deals that were so typical of the street life had to go through the family. Deals that didn't go through the family would, again, have a punishment that would result in a gruesome death. Certain police members were even bribed by these families in order to protect their business endeavors in the city. The police force typically abided in some shape or form out of greed and sometimes fear.

The Lucchese crime family had an order similar to other Mafia families at the time. Membership in this family was straightforward. A "made man" was one that could have his Italian descent traced back to the "homeland", as Italy was referred to by many. These men typically had groups within the family whom they controlled. A made man could not be touched, at least by the book standards. A made man could kill, ultimately, without question or reason if he felt it would advance or enable successful business. Clearly, made men had high influence and decision making power. An "associate" was a member of the crime family who did not have the full Italian lineage. While associates were not the ultimate decision-makers, these men still had vast amounts of power and stood on a step just slightly below a made man.

To expand this order further, families of the members were also awarded certain protections and exclusive rights. This has both pros and cons in the order of the Mafia. While families could thrive off of a luxurious lifestyle, protection from rivals, as well as having overall power, the negative actions or impacts of a member would commonly affect the members' whole family. In other words, if the family felt it was necessary to "whack", or kill, a member who had messed up or they needed gone, the entire family of that member would be in danger as well. These relationships and social order within the Lucchese family is crucial to understand in order to comprehend the path of Theresa Ferrara.

By 1972, Theresa Ferrara had been established in Queens for over 4 years. She was just 21 years old when she would meet a man that would change her ambitions forever. On a fateful night in Queens at one of the many Lucchese controlled bars, Ferrara was approached by Tommy DeSimone. Theresa was a highly attractive young woman, catching the eye of most any man she walked by. Tommy DeSimone was a married man. He was also a very powerful Lucchese family associate. The two soon would start an affair that would involve her in the Lucchese family affairs. All of the powerful players within the family quickly learned about Theresa. She was lavished with a lifestyle fit for a queen. While she and Tommy were not officially together, she was accepted into the lifestyle by this circumstance. She soon was a regular at the Lucchese hangouts. The infamous Robert's Lounge in downtown as well as The Suite, run by Henry Hill. She was quickly becoming involved in a life that was very familiar to her.

Over the next five years, Theresa Ferrara started making her money in much more daring ways than modeling. She quickly became a small quantity drug dealer. She was well known as a local cocaine and Quaalude dealer in the Lucchese owned areas of Queens. Not only did she sell drugs to every day residents of the area, she was selling drugs to Tommy DeSimone and other powerful Lucchese family members as well. This was obviously a risky endeavor. She even opened up her own MOB beauty salon in Bellmore, Long Island. In addition to doing Lucchese stylings, she was also selling drugs from her shop. While abiding by Mafia rules, she soon would attract unwanted attention. While some police officers could be bought, not all of them had a price tag. She was arrested in the summer of 1977 in her shop. She was charged on numerous counts of drug possession, smuggling, and distribution among many others. She would be facing a lengthy sentence. In just five years after entering the criminal lifestyle, she was facing the possibility of spending her best years in a jail cell. That is, if she couldn't find a way out of it.

Ferrara had been caught in the act. There wasn't a lawyer on the planet who could be successful in defending her charges. She had sold drugs out of her salon to an undercover Drug Enforcement Administration agent. Facing certain extended prison time, she agreed to cooperate with authorities. The Lucchese crime family was soon to be probed from within.

It was late in 1977 that Theresa Ferrara began to really gamble with her life. She knew that, as a cooperating witness who was feeding much needed evidence against the Mafia underworld, she would be afforded certain "protections" in her daily life from the FBI. Not only did she know this, she took great advantage of it. She began to rob many other successful salons in New York. The New York Police Department was forced to turn a blind-eye to this, as the FBI had abruptly ordered them to leave it alone. To law enforcement, getting the "big fish", in this case the Lucchese family, behind bars was priority number one, two, and three.

In 1978, Ferrara had begun to fully understand just how protected she was. When she had met Tommy DeSimone in 1972, she had immediately surrounded herself with numerous mob bosses and associates. Among these associates was a man named Richard Eaton. The significance of their relationship would come to a head in 1978, when he and Ferrara began to conspire to go after Lucchese money itself. The pair allegedly conspired to steal $250,000 worth of cocaine from a shipment that would arrive in Ft. Lauderdale, Florida. This was obviously a risky move, but by this time Theresa was fully working as a willing informant. It is crucial to remember that Theresa was not a member of the Lucchese family. While she had trust from the family due to her relationship with several associates, she did not have an integral role in the big operations that the family was executing. When Theresa conspired to steal from the Lucchese family, she was not acting on FBI orders. She was taking advantage of her government induced protection.

If this decision wasn't a risky enough gamble for Theresa, she had to go bigger. It was in December of 1978 when Ferrara and Eaton conspired to steal a hefty portion of the money stolen by the Lucchese family in the world famous Lufthansa Heist. Like many other crimes, the FBI could not solidly prove that this happened. It would essentially seem an odd coincidence that Ferrara moved to the North Shore Towers in Great Neck in January of 1979. This duplex would cost her $1500 per month just for rent. This was an extraordinary price for a 27 year old, single woman who was working in a salon and executing small time drug deals. If this seemed out of the ordinary for the people around her, it must have seemed very suspicious to the Lucchese family, especially at the time when money had disappeared and several deals had been tipped off to law enforcement. Even before the Lufthansa Heist, the family was becoming deeply suspicious of several people, perhaps none more than Theresa Ferrara.

Roughly a month before the famous Lufthansa Heist, Ferrara tipped off the FBI on a massive drug deal that was to go down. In November of 1978, the FBI and DEA brought down a drug smuggle of epic proportions. 30 tons of cocaine was intercepted at the Queens

Waterfront. Theresa Ferrara was solely responsible for tipping the agents off. The drug smugglers were said to be the Lucchese family leaders of Jimmy Burke, Paul Vario, and Tom Monteleone. The FBI had long wanted to take down Paul Vario, who was the financial brains it seemed of the family. Jimmy Burke was a powerful family boss who controlled a large area within the family reaches. Tom Monteleone was another boss for the family. These three men were furious when this shipment was intercepted. Paul Vario and Jimmy Burke were set to make $300,000 each off of this deal. This started suspicion among the entire family. The men knew there was a "rat" in their ranks. Even so, they were set to soon pull of one of the most notorious heist in United States history. This heist, ultimately, would cost Theresa Ferrara her life.

The Lufthansa Heist was an elaborate and well executed theft of enormous proportions. Depicted in many pop culture classics, these events go far beyond the crime itself. To understand the fall of Theresa Ferrara, the Lufthansa Heist is the single most important event to follow.

Lucchese crime family associate Jimmy Burke had planned the heist. Burke was easily one of the most powerful people in the Lucchese crime family, even though he could not be a "made man" due to his lineage. The heist planning started when Jimmy Burke's associate, the infamous Henry Hill, was given valuable information on millions of dollars in unmarked bills. These unmarked bills, as he was told, were flown in from West Germany once a month. This money was tourist money and as well as exchanges by military members of the region. The currency was flown in on a Lufthansa, the largest German airline for the time period. The money would then be stored in a vault at Kennedy Airport, where it would soon be transferred to its next destination. Jimmy Burke and Henry Hill were confident they could pull a heist off at the point just before the transfer from the vault. The informant, Louis Werner, was an airport worker who owed a Lucchese family book keeper, Martin Krugman, over $20,000 in gambling debts. Pleading for his life, Werner desperately gave this valuable, classified information to the family. The blue print for the plan had been set in motion. The execution would be one of the smoothest and skilled in United States history.

On December 11, 1979 the Lufthansa Heist began. At 3:12 A.M. cargo agent at the John F. Kennedy Airport noticed a black Ford van suspiciously backed up to the ramp door. He went over to investigate and was violently attacked. The two men, oddly not wearing any masks or gloves, pulled his hat over his eyes before hitting him multiple times in the head with pistols. He was thrown into the back of the van where another man was waiting for him.

"They threatened me. They told me they knew what I was about and that they knew where my family lived," cargo agent Kerry Whalen said. "They said they had others ready to go visit them."

With this chilling ultimatum, Whalen nodded his head to show that he understood. Senior agent Rolf Rebmann heard the noises that resulted coming from the loading ramp. He went out to investigate. He was met by six masked men brandishing powerful firearms. These men forced their way in and handcuffed Rebmann. Using a key that Werner had earlier provided, the men made their way with a bloodied Kerry Whalen and a handcuffed Rolf Rebmann through a maze of hallways and doors. They rounded up the two other employees and took them to the cafeteria. Information provided by the informant, Louis Werner, allowed the men to know what employees would be working and where they would be located. Without this information, it is likely they heist could not have worked.

There were six other employees eating their lunch in the cafeteria. The gunmen showcased the bloodied Kerry Whalen to the employees, perhaps in an effort to dissuade any of them of trying to resist. Nine of the ten employees were bound and gagged and made to lie on the cafeteria floor. One of the men, wielding a shotgun, was to keep look over these employees.

John Murray, another senior cargo agent, was forced to call Rudi Eirich on the intercom. Murray was forced, at gunpoint, to lead Eirich to believe there was a problem with the incoming load from Frankfurt. He was instructed to meet Murray in the cafeteria. This is significant to the Lucchese family because Rudi Eirich was the only security guard on duty that morning who knew the code to the double-door vault holding the money.

Eirich arrived to the cafeteria only to see all of the other employees bound and gagged on the floor as well as six men wielding shotguns. One man was to stay behind to keep eyes on the employees, while the other men took Eirich at gunpoint to the double-door vault.

Eirich would later testify as to how knowledgeable the men were to the vault. The double-door vault had a system to where both doors could not be unlocked at the same time. The robbers knew this and were very meticulous as to how they would continue the heist once inside the first door.

Rudi Eirich was forced to open the inner door first. This door led the robbers to a 10 ft. by 20 ft. room filled with all the goods they were seeking. There were hundreds of parcels available for the taking. Being as they were loading this into a single van, they had to make sure they took the right parcels. They searched through the invoices and freight records and decided on the packages they would take. They knew in all of this that if Eirich opened the second door, the alarm would sound. They bound Rudi to the floor as they executed the first part of their plan.

The men began to toss 40 parcels through the first door. This was done in less than 4 minutes. After this was complete, Eirich was untied and made to lock the inner door before unlocking the outer door. Once the inner door was locked and the outer door was opened, two of the men began to load the van with the 40 parcel haul. Eirich was again tied up and locked in the vault. With the van loaded, the men returned to the cafeteria at 4:14 A.M. They ordered the employees to call Port

Authority Police at 4:30 A.M. and not a second before. Having their lives and the lives of their families threatened, the employees obliged. The robbers left the employees at 4:16 A.M. The men left the airport, with all cash in tow in the van, at 4:21 A.M.

The Port Authority Police were not called until 4:30 A.M. This was crucial to the heist. Had they been called immediately when the robbers left, the building would have been under lock down within 90 seconds of the phone call. This information was valuable to the Lucchese family. This information was, again, obtained by the informant Louis Werner.

The robbers, having made an efficient and safe getaway, arrived at a garage in Canarsie, Brooklyn. Waiting for the van at the garage was none other than Jimmy Burke and his son Frank. The money was transferred from the van to another vehicle. This vehicle would be driven by Jimmy and Frank to one of the Lucchese family holdings. The other men were instructed to drive home. The driver of the get a way van, Parnell "Stacks" Edwards, was supposed to take the van used in the heist to a New Jersey auto yard and have the vehicle compacted and destroyed. When Jimmy and Frank arrived at the safe house to count the money, Jimmy was shocked by the haul. Expecting just over 2 million dollars, he was surprised to learn that the robbery had yielded them over 6 million dollars. This was the largest heist, at that point, on American soil ever recorded. To put the heist into another perspective, this was all achieved in just 64 minutes with no murders and no gun fire. Extensive planning and use of insider information led to one of the greatest crimes in history.

How does Theresa Ferrara fit into all of this? If she was an FBI informant at the time of the heist, why did she not tip off law enforcement? The events after the heist are nothing short of amazing. The murders that occurred at the hands of the original boss and leader of the heist were the direct result of paranoia. A key mistake made by Parnell "Stacks" Edwards would lead to the eventual murders of 10 integral members and perhaps dozens more that were not directly tied to the heist.

Jimmy Burke, Lucchese associate and crime ring leader, became increasingly suspicious of those around him. He was hell bent on eliminating anything or anyone that could lead police back to him for the heist. The year following the heist became known as the Witness Elimination Program. While not everyone was killed, anyone who made even the slightest misstep or raised any suspicion at all with Jimmy Burke was murdered. Police would be on a while goose chase from December 1978 to June 1979. The newspaper was regularly riddled with bodies, bloodshed, and mystery. The entire essence of organized crime in New York was facing the possibility of being completely dismembered as a result of the heist.

The key mistake made in the heist was, ironically, not a part of the heist itself. Parnell "Stacks" Edwards had a fairly simple job. He was the get a way driver of the van in a chase that never happened. He smoothly had to drive the fan to the garage. His main task was to get rid of the van after the transfer was made at the garage. Even for this, Jimmy told him exactly where to go and how simple the process would be. Not only did Edwards not take the van to the New Jersey auto yard for scraping, he didn't get rid of the van at all. He was obviously excited about the successful heist, and decided to celebrate by smoking marijuana on his way to the wrecking yard. In his confusion, he drove to his girlfriend's apartment and managed to leave the fan in a no parking zone. He spent the morning snorting cocaine and getting drunk with his girlfriend, fully intending to take the van to the auto yard later that day. Little to his knowledge, police had impounded the improperly parked van and quickly discovered it was the van used in the robbery. Edwards left the complex without being apprehended, however his fingerprints were found on the steering wheel. A muddy shoe print, found at the airport on the concrete surface, was matched with a shoe inside the van. This shoe also belonged to Edwards. For all intents and purposes, Parnell "Stacks" Edwards was officially a dead man walking.

The FBI, immediately following the heist, had narrowed it down between two major crime groups to blame for the Lufthansa Heist. The first group was the John Gotti crew, and the second was the Jimmy Burke crew. Burke had long had a reputation as a mastermind who was a stone cold murderer. The knowledge that was required to complete this heist led investigators to initially favor that it was, in fact, the work of Jimmy Burke and the Lucchese crime family. When Parnell "Stacks" Edwards made his mistake, police had the evidence they needed to go after the Jimmy Burke crew further. Edwards had long been a patron at Robert's Lounge, a well-known Burke gang hangout.

The FBI aggressively started a detailed procedure to investigate the Burke gang and try to gather enough evidence to obtain a warrant. They were constantly watching all of the known hangouts of Jimmy Burke and his crew. They bugged vehicles, tapped phone lines in establishments, and they even bugged the pay phones around the hang outs. They famously followed the gang in helicopters on numerous occasions. This was all common for Jimmy Burke and his gang in the months following the heist. Activity by police started as soon as the van was impounded in the days following the heist. This would trigger a deadly race between Jimmy Burke and the FBI. Jimmy knew that the police were on him, largely due to Edwards' mistake. Jimmy Burke would start a killing spree at this time in an effort to kill any witnesses and accomplices that he deemed suspicious. Parnell "Stacks" Edwards would be first.

Parnell "Stacks" Edwards was murdered execution style in his apartment just seven days after the heist. The shooters were two of Jimmy Burke's most trusted men: Tommy DeSimone and Angelo Sepe. These two men were largely believed to be involved in hundreds of murders over the years as ordered by Jimmy Burke and other Lucchese family associates. Angelo Sepe was believed to be the primary killer in the Witness Elimination murders as also ordered by Burke.

Tommy DeSimone, former boyfriend of Theresa Ferrara and valued member of the Jimmy Burke crew, was about to face the punishment for breaking the Mafia order. Earlier in 1978, DeSimone had murdered two valued "made men" of the Gambino crime family. Murdering made men was an especially deadly idea. No later than January 14, 1979, DeSimone was tricked into arriving at a Gambino location to be "made." Little did he realize, he was being lured in only to be assassinated. He was shot in the head and the face upon walking through the front door. Even worse for Jimmy Burke and the Lucchese family, they could not seek retribution for this as Tommy DeSimone had murdered "made men".

On February 10, 1979, Theresa Ferrara received a phone call at her salon from a caller that was unknown to all but Ferrara herself. "I have a chance to make $10,000," Ferrara told her 19-year-old niece Maria Sanacore. Theresa informed her that she was going to a nearby diner in Long Island. It struck Sanacore odd when Theresa told her that if she wasn't back in 15 minutes that she needed to come looking for her. Theresa Ferrara left the salon in a hurry, leaving behind her purse, car keys, and extravagant mink coat. This would be the last time she would be seen alive by anyone but her murderers.

On May 18, 1979, a female torso was found floating in Barnegat Inlet. This inlet is near Toms River, New Jersey and in the heart of much organized crime. The torso was not only dismembered completely, it was utterly unrecognizable. An extensive autopsy was performed. The body was identified through a recent breast augmentation. This was the body of Theresa Ferrara. No one has ever been convicted of the crime. There was simply no evidence. To understand who committed this, and why this was committed, it is important to understand the other murders in the Witness Elimination killings.

On January 6, 1979 Martin Krugman, the first to tip off Henry Hill and Jimmy Burke of the opportunity to plan the Lufthansa Heist, was murdered and dismembered in Vincent Asaro's fence factory. Hill later claimed that the remains of Krugman along with several others were buried under Robert's Lounge. Krugman was a book keeper for Jimmy Burke's gang and famously owned a wig shop and men's hair salon. He was ultimately murdered for his intense demands for his share of the heist money. Fearing that he would eventually tell investigators information on the heist, Burke had him killed.

On January 17, 1979 Richard Eaton was tortured and murdered by Jimmy Burke himself. Richard Eaton had teamed up with Theresa Ferrara earlier in 1978. Eaton was a con artist and an associate of Burke. He had no direct involvement in the Lufthansa Heist. He was caught with "fake cocaine" and running a scam while skimming money from the Lucchese family. Essentially, laundering money from the powerful family while selling a fake product. He also was skimming vast amounts of the Lufthansa Heist money using the same process. Theresa had proven involvement in this scam. She and Eaton had planned it out and knew what the Burke gang had done. The suspicion of the FBI is that Eaton, in an effort to save his own life, blamed the scam on Theresa Ferrara. In any event, the involvement of Ferrara and Eaton was known by the Lucchese family and Jimmy Burkes crew. His body was famously hanged in a meat freezer for investigators to find. This especially caught the attention of media and dominated headlines for many days in New York.

The next murder on the Witness Elimination timeline was that of Theresa Ferrara. She was next in line after her scam partner Richard Eaton. While still unsolved with no convictions, it is just one of several murders that happened in this killing spree with no solution. The Richard Eaton murder, however, would prove to have devastating consequences for Jimmy Burke.

In March 1979, the third accomplice of Theresa Ferrara and Richard Eaton was murdered in Florida. Tom Monteleone was accused of being involved in the scam as well, laundering the money through the Player's Club, a local bar that hosted Burke and his crew. This bar was owned by Monteleone.

The murders of Monteleone and Richard Eaton were essential evidence to FBI personnel that Jimmy Burke was responsible for the murder of Theresa Ferrara. However, they had no evidence and, with the subsequent murder of all the witnesses, would struggle to find the necessary evidence.

Over the next few months, five more witnesses would be murdered at the hands of Jimmy Burke and his crew. The effort he took to eliminate witnesses that could lead to his conviction in the heist was nearly successful. While most all of the murders were officially unsolved, there was one murder that could leave Jimmy Burke on a one-way trip to prison. That murder was none other than Richard Eaton's.

In 1982, Jimmy Burke was sentenced to 12 years in prison for his involvement in the Boston College point shaving scandal. While in prison, it is widely understood that many cohorts of Jimmy became more comfortable to talk. Through very secretive and reliable investigation, Jimmy Burke was charged with the murder of Richard Eaton while serving his 12 year prison term. He was sentenced to 20 years to life. Jimmy would eventually contract lung cancer and die in prison in 1996. He was 64 years old.

Henry Hill, the right hand man of Jimmy Burke, was largely the contributor to the ultimate murder conviction of Burke. Facing charges and a possibility of facing serious jail time, Hill cooperated with police. Henry Hill knew if he went to jail, his family was in serious danger. For his information, Henry Hill was admitted to the Witness Protection Program with his family. He died in 2012.

The fates of nearly all of those involved in the heist were dreadful. While murders were confirmed by police, more than half of the slain bodies were never found. The bodies that were found typically were put in place because the Mafia families wanted them found. Most of the money obtained in the heist was predictably put back in to the streets or in casinos or drugs. While police didn't solve most of these murders, the perpetrators usually received their own fates by other members. To pull off one of the most lucrative heist in history, there is understandably going to be collateral damage. However, this amount of damage was near total.

Theresa Ferrara was just 27 years old when she was murdered. Pursuing a modeling and acting career, she moved to Queens. Her story, while one of tragedy and sadness, is largely a result of her own decisions. Ultimately, she tried to scam one of the most powerful families in New York, and her fate was sealed. The nature of chasing a dream and living a lifestyle is a complicated one. Who you surround yourself with will largely determine your lifestyle. For Theresa Ferrara, she surrounded herself with MOB associates and criminal bosses, and eventually she was dealt a hand that she wouldn't survive.

JUAN RAUL GARZA : MEXICAN DRUG LORD

AIMEE CLARK

Juan Raul Garza

Juan Raul Garza was born in Brownsville, Texas on November 18, 1957. On June 19, 2001, he was executed by lethal injection at the United States Penitentiary in Terra Haute, Indiana. He was the second murderer executed by the US government since 1963. Timothy McVeigh – responsible for 168 deaths in the Oklahoma City bombing – was the first, preceding Garza by a mere eight days.

In his 44 years on earth, Garza married a woman – Elizabeth – who would stand by him no matter what he did. Together, they had four children – Juan Jr, Elizabeth (after her mother), Maribel, and Norma – who were close to their father and loved him unconditionally. "He will always be my daddy," said Norma Garza at her father's sentencing.

He also built and controlled an intricate drug trafficking enterprise, having a hand in at least three murders. However, it is believed he played some part in another five killings – including that of his son-in-law – for which he was never tried.

His sentence and execution was one that sparked controversy and raised questions of racial inequality. As Garza's attorney is noted as saying after his execution, "A white man had to kill over 150 people to be put to death by the United States Government but this Hispanic man only had to have a hand in 3 murders to receive the same treatment."

Drugs, Money, & Murder

Early in the 1980s, Garza along with friends and associates from the tough neighborhood he grew up in began to build a lucrative drug trafficking enterprise. They moved thousands of pounds of marijuana throughout Texas, Louisiana, and Michigan.

Garza's fledgling organization began by selling drugs that other smugglers would bring into the country. As his organization grew, Garza began sending men of his own in to Mexico to bring the marijuana into the US. Hundreds of thousands of dollars were earned in return.

That amount would have been even more had it not been for the occasional setbacks when loads of drugs and cash were seized by law enforcement agencies. These incidents put a sizable dent in Garza's profits. They also left him suspicious of those closest to him.

For at least three men, that suspicion proved deadly.

The first man to fall prey to Juan Garza's suspicion was Gilberto Matos. Matos was an associate of fellow drug smuggler Erasmo De La Fuente. Garza believed De La Fuente was responsible for the tip that led police to a 1350-pound shipment of marijuana that was seized from one of Garza's warehouse storage locations.

Garza sent some of his henchmen to murder De La Fuente but they were unable to get to the man due to his entourage. The small group of men – including bodyguards and Matos – accompanied De La Fuente everywhere.

Sick of waiting for a chance to get De La Fuente alone, Garza ordered Manuel Flores and his cousin Israel Flores to lay a trap. They were to break into Matos' auto repair shop and lie in wait for either De La Fuente or Matos. If only Matos arrived then they were to kill him as a warning to De La Fuente.

When Matos entered his shop alone, Israel and Manuel forced him to lie face down on the floor. They held him there for nearly an hour in the hope that De La Fuente would appear. When he did not and they grew tired of waiting, they shot Matos in the back of the head and left the scene.

As payment, Garza gave Israel and Manuel an unknown amount of money and a car.

Not yet ready to give up his vendetta against De La Fuente, Garza gave Israel Flores and his brother Jesus guns and personally drove them to De La Fuente's nightclub to kill him. Israel got too drunk to help with the murder and was dropped off in an alley nearby.

After dropping off his brother, Jesus Flores picked up their cousin Manuel and returned to De La Fuente's nightclub to finish the hit. They lay in wait until De La Fuente exited the club and got into his car. That was when Manuel stepped out of the dark and shot him twice through the driver's side window.

Jesus fired shots into the air at random to distract onlookers and police from Manuel as he ran from the scene. He then hid in a ditch for a few hours until the heat died down. He called Garza and was picked up shortly afterward.

Each of the Flores' was paid $10,000 for the hit.

The third victim was Thomas Rumbo. After being caught loading marijuana into a trailer, Rumbo agreed to cooperate with police and turned the entire 360-pound shipment over to officers. In an effort to conceal his betrayal and save his life, Rumbo told Garza's men that the drugs had been stolen and cut a hole in the fence that surrounded the trailer to help his alibi look more credible.

Garza was not fooled. He took two of his men and went straight to Rumbo's house believing that the man had stolen the drugs himself. The three men convinced Rumbo to get into Garza's pickup truck and they drove to the home of another of the kingpin's associates. Here – unbeknownst to Rumbo – Garza picked up a gun.

They made another stop at the home of Jesus Flores who owed Garza money for cocaine. Jesus volunteered to go along and five men – Kingpin Juan Garza, Thomas Rumbo, henchman Jesus Flores, and two associates of Garza's that they picked up at the last stop – all got into Flores' car.

Jesus Flores interrogated Rumbo as they drove around but the man did not waver from his story. Frustrated, Garza drove out to a rural farm road and told Rumbo that he knew the man had stolen his marijuana.

Told to walk home, Rumbo climbed out of the car. It is unlikely that he had any idea what hit him as Garza shot him in the back of the head before he had finished exiting the vehicle. The man fell lifelessly back into the car and was dragged unceremoniously into some nearby bushes where Garza shot his dead body four more times in a fit of rage.

The Noose Tightens

Law enforcement agents gradually tightened the noose around Garza's operations. His phones were tapped and they surveilled his activities closely. More loads of drugs and money were seized costing Garza profits and respect. As more and more of Garza's associates and henchmen were arrested and converted to informants the end of Garza's empire of crime loomed near.

Garza himself was arrested at one point after making a delivery to an undercover agent in person.

In February of 1992, an assault helicopter, hundreds of federal agents, and an S.W.A.T. team descended on the homes and businesses of Garza and his associates. The U. S. Customs Service secured and searched all of them.

As a result, almost all of Garza's associates – included all three of the Flores men – were arrested and indicted. Garza, however, escaped to Mexico before he could be found.

The indictment originally named Garza and 15 of his co-conspirators on two counts of drug trafficking. However, since Garza was unable to be found due to his flight to Mexico the government made plea agreements with the majority of these co-conspirators. They were allowed to plea to lesser charges in exchange for their testimony against Juan Raul Garza.

Garza was finally located when he ran out of money and contacted a former associate in Michigan to try to arrange a sale. The man was secretly working with the authorities and agreed to let them tape record his conversations with Garza. The calls were traced and the Mexican government apprehended Garza at his hideout and turned him over to U. S. Customs Agents.

After all the plea agreements were made, Garza was reindicted, this time on ten counts. They include five counts of violations of various drug trafficking laws, one count of operating a continuing criminal enterprise (CCE), one count of money laundering, and three counts of killing in furtherance of a CCE.

Conviction & Sentencing

In 1993, Juan Raul Garza was tried and convicted of all ten of the counts on which he was indicted. Due to the fact that all of his criminal activities were tied to drug offenses, he was tried under the guidelines of the 1988 Federal Anti-Drug Act.

At the sentencing hearing, the same jury that had found Garza guilty handed down his sentence. He received three concurrent terms of imprisonment for life for count one – conspiracy to import more than 1,000 kilograms of marijuana into the U.S. from Mexico – count two – conspiracy to possess with intent to distribute more than 1,000 kilograms of marijuana – and count six. Two 40-year sentences were handed down for count three – possession with intent to distribute approximately 163.6 kilograms of marijuana – and count five – possession with intent to distribute approximately 596.3 kilograms of marijuana. Two twenty year sentences were given for count four – possession with intent to distribute approximately 95.4 kilograms of marijuana – and count 10.

For counts seven, eight, and nine – the three murder charges –, the jury sentenced Juan Raul Garza to death. That sentence would make Garza the first person put to death under the 1988 Federal Anti-Drug Abuse Act, which imposed a death sentence for murders stemming from a drug enterprise.

During Garzas sentencing hearing, witnesses testified about three more shooting deaths Garza ordered in Mexico, and a fourth he committed personally. The four allegedly killed in Mexico included Garza's son-in-law, Bernabe Sosa, whose body was found Jan. 22, 1992; Oscar Cantu, a pilot whose body was found in April 1992; and

Antonio Nieto and Fernando Escobar Garcia, whose bodies were found in May 1991.

In closing arguments during the trial, prosecutors referred to Sosa's death. "He corrupts (his family members) and eventually kills them, like he did Bernabe Sosa, his own son-in-law," a prosecutor said at the trial.

Garza was never charged with the four deaths in Mexico but Jose Maria Sosa, Bernabe Sosa's brother told The Brownsville Herald in a recent interview that all evidence points to Garza because Maribel Sosa, Bernabe's wife, left her husband with Garza the day he disappeared.

It was these unproven claims – among several other things – that led groups such as the ACLU (American Civil Liberties Union) and the Inter-American Commission on Human Rights to take up Garza's cry for appeal.

Appeals & Controversy

According to the ACLU fact sheet for Juan Garza, the jury that sentenced Garza to death was told repeatedly by the federal prosecutor that if he was not sentenced to death Garza could be released from prison in as little as twenty years. This was not true.

Under the Federal Sentencing Guidelines, the jury could have sentenced Garza to life in prison without the possibility of release. The ACLU points out that Juan Garza is the only inmate on federal death row whose jury did not receive the "life in prison without the possibility of release" option.

Garza's attorneys – and the groups supporting him – believe that if the jury had been given this instruction, Garza's life may have been spared. They cite a factually similar case that took place in Michigan – U. S. v. Bass – where 11 death eligible defendants were prosecuted for four gang related murders and the jury sentenced all four defendants to live imprisonment.

Raising this concern in their many appeals, Garza's attorneys made no progress in getting his sentencing examined again. This time with consideration given to the possibility of a sentence of life in prison without the possibility of release. This is despite the fact that a similar case in South Carolina – Shafer v. South Carolina – in March of 2001 the trial court's failure to properly instruct the jury was an ruled an unconstitutional error by the U. S. Supreme Court.

Originally scheduled for December 12, 2000, Garza's execution was delayed just five days before it was supposed to occur when President Clinton intervened during his last days in office by granting him a six month reprieve "to allow the Justice Department time to gather an properly analyze more information about racial and geo graphic disparities in the federal death penalty system."

President Clinton's decision was based largely upon the Justice Department's federal death penalty report. Released in September of 2000, the results of an internal survey ordered by the then Attorney General (AG) Janet Reno. It revealed stark racial and regional disparities in the application of the death penalty in federal cases. Of the 20 people on the federal death row, 85% – which boils down to 17 people – were minorities with the racial breakup being 14 Black, 3 Hispanic, and 3 White.

Further, between 1995 and 2000, 80% of all federal cases submitted for the death penalty involved minority defendants. During that period, defendants were allowed to plead guilty in exchange for a life sentence in only 32% of the cases. When compared to the percentage of each ethnic group that entered guilty pleas, the report concluded that white defendants were much more likely to escape the death sentence through a plea bargain.

In addition, the federal death penalty is geographically arbitrary since only a handful of judges pursue it. Cases prosecuted in the southern states of Texas, Virginia, Oklahoma, Alabama, Florida,

Louisiana, and Georgia accounted for 65% of the total federal death penalty cases.

When looked at together, the facts presented in the Justice Department report make it seem as though being of a minority race in those seven southern states all but guarantees a death penalty sentence.

President Clinton reviewed the report and concluded that "the examination of possible racial and regional bias should be completed before the U. S. goes forward with an execution in a case that may implicate the very questions raised by the Justice Department's continuing study. In this area there is no room for error."

However, on May 30th, the U. S. Court of Appeals for the 5th Circuit denied Garza's motion for a delay. In response, Juan Garza's attorneys asked the new President, George Bush to commute Garza's sentence to life in prison without the chance of release.

During his confirmation hearings as President George H. W. Bush's new Attorney General, John Ashcroft agreed with Clinton's assessment. He said that there was "a need for 'continuing study' of possible racial and regional bias in the federal death penalty," and that "a thorough study of the system" was warranted. However, on June 6th, Ashcroft did a 180 and completely changed his tune. Saying at that time that there was, "no evidence of bias against racial or ethnic minorities" and that he would not authorize any further study of the matter.

In relation to the case of Juan Raul Garza, Ashcroft said, "I know of no reason not to proceed with the Garza execution."

A group of prominent Americans that went by the name Citizens for a Moratorium on Federal Executions were the ones who successfully petitioned President Clinton on behalf of Garza. They sent an open letter to President Bush asking the President to declare "an immediate moratorium on all federal executions.

Among the people who signed the letter were Artist Harry Belafonte; the Chair on the U. S. Commission on Civil Rights, Dr.

Mary Frances Berry; Cardinal Roger Mahoney, Archbishop of the Roman Catholic Archdiocese in Los Angeles, federal congressional representatives, and state attorney generals.

Bush refused to grant Garza clemency after two Supreme Court rulings against Garza. White House spokesperson, Ari Fleischer said, "The president found no grounds to grant clemency in this case."

In a report compiled by the Bush administration Justice Department, "no racial or regional bias was found in the federal death penalty law." This, obviously, is in direct opposition to the report released by the Clinton administration Justice Department less than a year earlier. The new Justice Department stated that a "recently completed study" (of which no details could be found or offered) is the source of their findings.

An attorney for Garza, John Howley strongly disagreed saying, "There's no question that race plays a big part in every death sentence. The fact is we only give out the death penalty in this country to poor, to minorities, and to the mentally retarded."

Gregory Wiercioch, an attorney for Garza, said that an upcoming report on the death penalty by the Attorney General John Ashcroft would someday be placed on the shelves next to the Dred Scott decision and Plessy v Ferguson, "as a shameful attempt to justify the unjustifiable."

"Someday, this precise savagery will end, but not today," Wiercioch, said. "Today President Bush had the last word. But he will not have the final say on the death penalty. History will."

Death penalty opponents – and even some former Justice Department officials – have often voiced the theory that Garza would be alive today, serving an life sentence without the chance for parole, if he had committed his crimes somewhere other than Texas and if he had been white.

They point to the fact that six of the 19 men currently on federal death row were sentenced in Texas ... that is over 30%. Moreover, 17 of those 19 men – including all six of the men from Texas – are minorities ... that is a whopping 90%!

Robert Litt, former deputy assistant attorney general during the Clinton administration, said, "There is a question of whether the way the system is set up produces arbitrary and discriminatory results. I think somebody ought to get some answers and understand what is going on."

During his last day on earth, Juan Raul Garza spent the day reading, resting, watching television, and visiting with his attorneys. Garza also had a meeting with the warden who explained what the inmate could expect in his final hours. He ordered a final meal that consisted of a rare steak, French fries, onion rings, three slices of bread, and a diet cola ... that must have been out of habit as his weight was no longer something about which Garza needed to worry.

Execution

At 7:09 a.m. on June 19, 2001, just two days after visiting with his wife and children for Father's Day, Juan Raul Garza was executed by lethal injection. His death was certainly more merciful than any of the murders he had been a part of but by many it was considered just as unjust.

His final words contained an apology for "the pain and grief I have caused" both to his victims and his own family. "I just want to say that I am sorry, and I apologize for all the pain and grief that I have caused," he said. "I ask your forgiveness and God bless."

Strapped to the same gurney that McVeigh had died on a little over a week before, Warden Harley Lappin remembers Garza nervously flexing his feet as Lappin tied the curtains back on the witness rooms.

Dan Dunne, U. S. Bureau of Prisons spokesperson, said that the scene was a stark contrast to that of the week before when Timothy McVeigh met the same fate. For one thing, there were only a handful of people protesting, and they were protesting the death penalty in general, not seeking clemency for McVeigh in particular. In addition, more than 1000 reporters requested credentials to cover the Oklahoma City domestic terrorist being executed. Conversely, only about 75 reporters applied to cover the execution of Juan Garza.

As the chemicals entered Garza's veins, he slowly closed his eyes and passed into a peaceful eternal slumber. Outside, more than 50 protestors futilely sang songs and held signs demanding the execution stop.

A journalist from the Tribune - Star newspaper in Terre Haute, Indiana – where the execution took place – was one of the media representatives who witnessed Juan Garza's execution. At a news conference that followed, Karen Grunden described the execution in detail.

"When we walked into the media witness room, the curtains were still closed. There are two windows in that room, and a metal bar that comes out from eh window area that prevents us from getting up right close to the window. It was a bluish green curtain. It opened at approximately 7:00 a. m. today. We saw Mr. Garza on the gurney. He had a white sheet draped on him, draped down to the floor, to about here. And there was a white sheet on the gurney underneath him, as well. You could see that he was wearing a white tee shirt.

"The warden did walk by our window right after the curtain had opened. And Mr. Garza seemed to look at someone, possibly, in this inmate witness room and give a nod before the drugs were administered, before he gave his final statement. He did look around a little bit, seemed to look at each of the rooms a bit, just to kind of gauge who was there, and was given his opportunity to make the final statement. You have already heard that.

"The sentencing information was read by Warden Lappin, and it was three counts of intentional killing in a criminal conspiracy, I believe – something to that effect.

"His hair was graying a bit. He did blink a few times, and this was after the first drug, apparently, had already started. He looked again at the inmate witness room, and as he laid there, his eyes, at the end, did look towards the ceiling, but his head was tilted toward that inmate witness room so that he could kind of look in there.

"He did swallow. His eyes became drowsy. There was not really a point at any time where you could actually say he died. There was no final breath that we noticed at all. Someone had said that his feet had moved. His eyes were still open, but his left eye seemed to droop more closed than the other one.

"The time of death, as has been said, was 7:09."

Conclusion

Juan Raul Garza was not a good man. His family loved him so we can believe that there was some part of him that was good, as there is with every other person. However, for the most part, the Mexican-American boy born to migrant workers in Texas grew up to be an extremely bad man.

Bringing drugs into the country and distributing them throughout the communities of at least three different states, extortion, bribery, theft, brutal violence, and even murder were not too much for Juan Garza. He was willing to do anything he had to in the pursuit of money and power.

In the end, he destroyed not only his own life, but also the lives of everybody around him. Associates that he brought into the seedy underbelly of society to help him in his endeavors are in jail or murdered by his own hand. His family was left without a father and provider in addition to being nearly penniless due to the government's seizure of all of his assets as forfeitures under the drug law.

The people he murdered or ordered killed and all of the people in their lives that depended upon them and loved them, also had their lives ruined by Garza. Those whose lives were destroyed by the drugs Garza funneled into the country can also trace their downfall to him.

His friends were safe but only because they were nonexistent. Garza surrounded himself with lackeys, henchmen, and other people that served a practical purpose in his business ... or risked joining his list of dead associates.

The web of destruction wrought by Garza's selfish and criminal enterprises extends across the entire United States touching more than just the people who knew he existed.

While it is still questionable whether Garza got a sentencing, the fact of the matter is as Bush's Attorney General, John Ashcroft said, "The guilt of Juan Raul Garza is not in question." He definitely committed the crimes.

The only question is ... did he deserve to die for those crimes?